EXPLORE YOUR DESTINY
WITH RUNES

EXPLORE YOUR DESTINY WITH RUNES

REVEAL THE SECRETS OF YOUR FUTURE WITH THIS ANCIENT DIVINATION SYSTEM

Joanna Sandsmark

A GODSFIELD BOOK
www.godsfield.co.uk

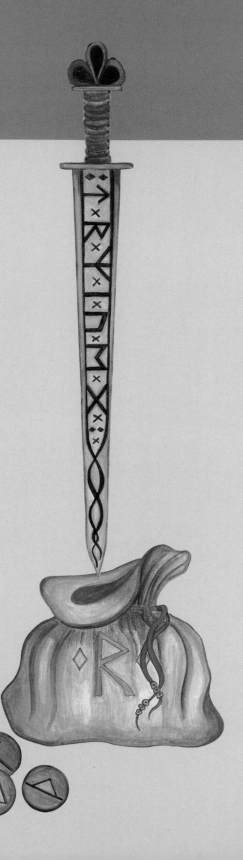

Dedicated to the Bats.

First published in Great Britain in 2006 by
Godsfield Press, a division of Octopus Publishing Group Ltd
2–4 Heron Quays, London E14 4JP

ISBN-10: 978-184181-305-9
ISBN-13: 1-84181-305-2

A CIP catalogue record for this book is available from the
British Library

Printed and bound in China

10 9 8 7 6 5 4 3 2 1

CONTENTS

UNDERSTANDING RUNES

Before you can begin to use runes for any sort of divination, you will need

to learn about their origins, associations and history. Then you can move

on to making a set of your own, and discovering how to work with them.

INTRODUCTION

Germanic tribes in northern Europe used runes to communicate via the written word. Runes were an alphabet, but they were also a connection to their gods and a source of mystery and divination. Intricately carved rune stones can still be found throughout northern Europe, and beyond.

It is possible that the magical aspects of runes came before their use as the symbols of language. One can imagine a shaman of a Germanic tribe scratching mysterious symbols onto pieces of wood, and using them to guard his people against attack, famine, drought and all manner of negative happenings. Soon, those symbols would take on greater meanings. That is what alphabets are: symbols that allow us

to communicate with one another in rich and complex ways.

The runic alphabet, or 'futhark' (a word that stands for the first six runes, F, U, Th, A, R and K), consists of symbols that are not just used to create words – they also have fully realized meanings in and of themselves. If you use the letter 'f' in a word, it stands for a sound and holds a place in that word. With the runes, Fehu has a sound and a place, but it also stands for cattle and wealth. This adds a further dimension to runic writing that is both foreign and thrilling. The layers of meaning are rife with possibilities.

Now add one more aspect and you will clearly see the appeal of runes: they are

also magical. The word 'rune' means secret or mystery. Methods of magic have been created throughout our world. From astrology to palmistry, Tarot to I-Ching, divination has always held a fascination for humankind. Now you, too, have a little magic at your fingertips. It's an intriguing idea, isn't it?

HOW TO USE THIS BOOK

The book is divided into three parts: 'Understanding runes', 'Reading runes' and 'Using runes for positive change'. In the rest of this first part, you will learn about the origins of runes, how to make your own set of runes and how to work with them, including making a rune pouch, drawing or casting your stones, and how to create and keep a rune journal.

The second part contains a complete colour-coded listing of the runes, showing what the symbols look like, what they are called and what they mean in a runecast, both upright and reversed. This is the heart of the book and contains the pages with which you will want to familiarize yourself in order to do your readings.

You will find further help in the last part, because it introduces you to several layouts, numerous searching self-questions and also takes you through a number of sample readings. When you have finished the book, you'll have all the tools you need to begin your journey as a runecaster.

ORIGINS

According to the *Poetic Edda*, a collection of Norse poetry, the runes came to mankind from Odin, who sacrificed himself by hanging from the life tree, Yggdrasil, for nine days. As a reward for his sacrifice, he received the knowledge of the runes. It is a great origin story, with a sacrificing god, torment and pain, all wrapped up in mysticism and arcane knowledge. It also shows how important the runes were to the people who used them. When something comes through the sacrifice of the king of your gods, you know it has to be pretty special. The runes lived up to their hype.

Yet, as wonderful as that story is, the 'real-world explanation' is much more down to earth. Runes first began appearing among Germanic people around 200 BC. There are questions as to whether they adapted some of the symbols from the Roman, Greek or Etruscan alphabets, or if they were more pictographic in nature, like the hieroglyphics of Egypt. There are, in fact, several theories about the origins of the runes, none of which has been proven or holds the opinion of the majority of experts.

It is fitting that the word 'rune' means mystery, in light of this scholarly debate. The truth is probably buried in antiquity, as any good mystery should be. What is known is that the runes were not static symbols, unchanged through a millennium. There are several versions of the futhark, from the Elder Futhark (which will be used in this book) to the Nordic, English and Celtic versions, and more.

In the variations, individual letters change their shapes, some are added, others subtracted; but, at heart, they are all runic systems of writing. They were carved on stones or wood to tell the story of a heroic deed, mark the grave of a fallen comrade or even as graffiti, written by a smitten Viking pining for the blonde beauty who awaited his return.

VARIATIONS ON A THEME

The Elder Futhark with its 24 symbols was divided into three families, or 'aettir', of eight runes apiece. The first family, or 'aett', begins with Fehu and ends with Wunjo; the second begins with Hagalaz and ends with Sowilo; and the third starts with Tiwaz and ends at Othala. The first eight stones are about creation, the second are the human elements and the last is the journey to god- or goddesshood. Note that the blank rune, Wyrd (pronounced 'weird'), is a modern addition and not part of the Elder Futhark's 24 symbols.

This neat division into groups of eight changed when the futhark spread from its origins in the Germanic tribes. When the Anglo-Saxons began using the runes, they added some new ones and changed the look of some of the old ones. The Scandinavians did the opposite – they eliminated several runes, paring down their futhark to only 16 stones.

Today, there are various names to describe the different rune lines, including the Anglo-Frisian Futhark, the Younger Futhark, the Armonen Futhork, and so on. This is why you will occasionally see differences in both the shapes and names of the runic symbols in various texts. It is not that any one shape or name is right and the others are wrong; nor does it affect the magic of the symbols. All it really does is deepen the sense of mystery that surrounds the runes.

Don't worry if the terms are confusing – all those words such as futhark, aettir and Fehu can tie up the tongue fairly quickly if you are not familiar with Scandinavian languages. This is an introductory book and so my goal is not to confuse you or go into long passages of scholarly research. To get any understanding of the runes, however, you do need to know some of the language surrounding them. My advice is to let the terms wrap around your tongue and to delight in their musical beauty.

RUNES OF ROMANCE

Runes were often carved onto sticks, and sent with runners. These runners with runic staves were the postal system of that ancient world. Some of these ancient 'letters' still survive. After a terrible fire destroyed parts of the wharf area of Bergen, Norway, in 1955, excavators found an enormous cache of rune-covered wooden sticks and slates dating from the early middle ages. They were on a wide

range of subjects such as business and trade, politics, ship manifests and religion (primarily Christian at that time).

There were also scores of personal letters and notes. 'My darling, kiss me,' begged a runic love letter. The writer added the entire futhark after his note, to ensure that his message had plenty of magic. On a more practical level, the note that proclaimed 'Gyda says that you are to go home' might have been a message from an angry wife to a philandering husband.

Love spells and romantic messages are as old as humanity and the runes have a strong history in this area. From secret erotic rites, where participants formed the

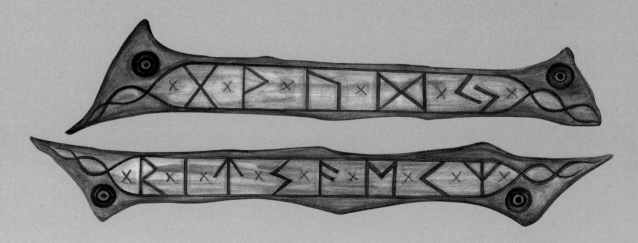

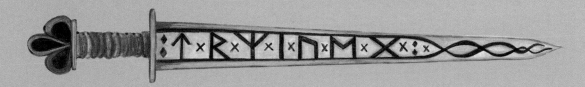

images of the runes as sexual positions, to romantic Viking swains who begged the object of their desire to 'Think of me, I am thinking of you. Love me, I love you' in flowing lines of runes, the futhark has had a powerful influence. When you read about the rune Gebo, you will see that this X-shaped rune is still in use today as the 'kiss' at the bottom of a letter or love note.

THE VIKINGS

Runes also held power in hunting rituals and war. Vikings carved them on their swords, shields and helmets, hoping for their powerful protection. Runes on the shaft of an arrow were thought to help the arrow find its mark.

It does not take a big leap of imagination to go from carving a rune on your shield to etching them onto bits of wood as oracles to portend the future. The ancient shamans who knew the way of the runes shared cryptic hints about their meanings in poetry. The Vikings were especially fond of poetry. Based not on rhyme, but on rhythmic alliteration and using cryptic riddles knows as 'kennings', Viking poetry in its original tongue is both stirring and beautiful. Several poems were devoted to the esoteric meanings of the runes and they have survived to this day.

The Viking age, which lasted from approximately AD 800 to 1100, was the zenith of rune use. As the Vikings

left Scandinavia to conquer other lands, they took their language and the futhark with them. From Greenland and Iceland to the British Isles, France and Russia, rune stones can still be found, left as a calling card by Viking warriors and explorers.

END OF AN ERA AND A NEW BEGINNING

When the Viking age ended, owing to the rise of Christianity, the pagan implications of the runes were no longer in favour. As a result, rune lore was nearly wiped out. There was no place in a Christian world for symbols that held magical qualities. They might have died out altogether if a few Scandinavians had not kept them alive in isolated villages.

In the 17th century, there was a resurgence in the popularity of the runes, but it did not last long. The late 19th and early 20th centuries saw another rise in interest, culminating in Hitler's Nazi party adopting several runes as symbols. As you can imagine, this set things back again once World War II ended. But, when memories began to fade, the runes returned and have enjoyed a renaissance to the present day.

There are several excellent volumes written about the runes, their history, both real and esoteric, and the people who used them. If you find your curiosity triggered, then you will have a great many resources from which you can draw more detailed information. It is my hope that this introductory volume will lead you to greater study of this fascinating oracle.

HOW DO THEY WORK?

If, when using this book, you begin to wonder how runes can be so uncannily accurate time after time, I have to admit that I don't know the answer. It might be your own inner wisdom that chooses the stones, all-knowing and all-powerful. It might be the synchronicity of nature, providing you with guidance simply because you need that message at that time. It could be that the electric and chemical components in your human 'engine' react to the positive or negative charges of the stones. Or it might just be that the runes truly are magic!

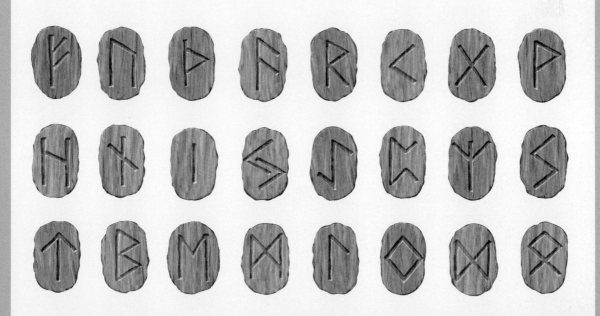

The first thing you are going to need is a set of runes. There are several ways to accomplish this. If you don't want to expend a lot of effort, you can purchase runes. If you have access to a computer connected to the internet, use a search engine to locate a website that sells runes. If you live in a city or a town, there might be speciality shops in your area that stock them. Buying runes may be the easiest method, but if you want your set to be imbued with your own essence, then by far the best way is to make them yourself.

You may have heard runes referred to as 'stones' or 'rune stones'. This is a convenient way to indicate the physical object upon which the runic symbol is painted or carved. I will carry on this tradition in this text. It does not mean that your runes have to be made of stone. In fact, most people make their first set of runes out of wood, which is a traditional material for making 'rune stones'.

Wood, stone and bone are all things found in nature and help to connect the runes to their spiritual source. The gods and goddesses of the ancient Germanic and Norse peoples played a key role in the lives of their worshippers, and the runes embody these deities in some ways. To preserve that connection to nature and to the ancients, I encourage you to consider making a set of runes out of natural materials.

WOOD

Perhaps the best material, and the easiest to work with, is wood. If you have access to natural wood (a tree that wouldn't mind giving up a branch), then that is ideal. Before cutting, say a prayer of thanks to the tree for giving you the gift of one of its branches. If you like, you can give an offering to the tree in exchange. A gift of water or fertilizer, or the burial of one of its seeds, would certainly do.

Some rune experts recommend fruit trees, but it is more important that the wood is one you personally want to hold and work with. If you have always felt strongly about oak or maple, for example, or if you prefer yew or pine, then seek one of these woods first.

If tree branches are not available, you can go to any wood or timber merchants and buy a piece of dowelling. The piece of wood should have a diameter of approximately 2.5 cm (1 in). You want to be able to hold all your runes in your hands, so keep the size comfortable for you. You can either trim the bark off the branch, or leave it

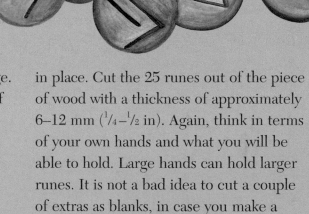

in place. Cut the 25 runes out of the piece of wood with a thickness of approximately 6–12 mm ($^1/_4$–$^1/_2$ in). Again, think in terms of your own hands and what you will be able to hold. Large hands can hold larger runes. It is not a bad idea to cut a couple of extras as blanks, in case you make a mistake or lose one of your runes.

Once you have cut the discs, use sandpaper to soften any rough edges. You are going to be handling these wooden discs, so they need to be tactically pleasing. Getting splinters is not in the forecast! When you have finished sanding all 25 discs, you are ready to make your runes. There are several ways you can imprint the symbols onto the wooden blanks. You can use a wood-burning tool to sear the shape, or you can use a knife or chisel to carve the rune. Some people don't agree with the idea of further harming the wood by burning it and carving can be both tricky and dangerous; so, if you choose either of those options, it is best if you are already skilled in the craft. Another option is to paint the symbols onto the wood.

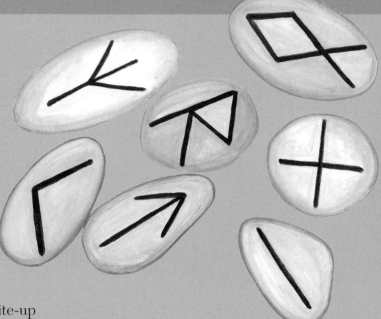

Pick up a disc and look at the write-up for Fehu, the first rune in the futhark. Say the name out loud, and think about what it means. Once you feel you are ready, burn, carve or paint the symbol onto the blank face of the disc. Continue doing this until you have finished all 24 runes, leaving a 25th disc blank, for the rune Wyrd.

Congratulations! You have a set of runes. You are the one who made these runes. You found the wood, cut them, formed them, burned, carved or painted their symbols onto them, and imbued them with your essence. Because of this process, they are now a source of power for you.

STONE

Stones are also popular. They make a wonderful clinking sound in your rune bag, and, if polished, are very tactile. I own a set of polished malachite runes that are quite beautiful. I smile whenever I see them, and that alone helps to imbue them with part of my joyful spirit.

To make your own set of stone runes, you will need to gather or purchase the stones you want to use. Although it is best to have runes that are all the same shape and size, that gets a little difficult with stones. Just make sure they are all approximately the same size.

Use paint on your stone runes, because chiselling onto such a small surface would be both difficult and dangerous. Choose a paint that will show up and won't chip. Follow the same ritual as outlined in the 'wood' section above.

BONE

There are many examples of ancient texts that refer to Nordic or Germanic people 'casting bones'. Some even describe sets of bone tokens with symbols carved upon them. It stands to reason that bone would be a natural choice with which to make your runes. However, this will depend on your own feelings about using parts of a

dead animal for divination. Would those runes be infused with death? Would they hold some of the strength and life force of the animal to which they once belonged? Would there be some sort of influence on the runes that would fight your own life force when doing a reading? If you are unsure of the answers, or don't have an immediate reaction, positive or negative, to using bone, it would be best for you to meditate on the answers to these and any questions that might come up.

If you do decide to use bone then you must consider which animal would best serve you. For example, if you like the idea of using bone but don't want the material associated with death, you could look for the antlers of any species of deer or elk. They shed their antlers once a year. If you have access to any discarded antlers, they hold no traces of death. In some cultures they are a symbol of rebirth.

The preparation of bone or antler runes should be carried out in the same way as for wooden runes.

OTHER MATERIALS

With imagination and perhaps some special talents, you can make your runes in other ways. If you have access to a kiln, then making them from clay, in uniform sizes, is an excellent alternative. You can carve the symbols before the clay is fired, and use glazes or paint to add to their beauty. Be sure that you use genuine clay, and not a synthetic version, because the runes must be made from natural materials.

If you are a metal-worker, you can make runic jewellery. If there is one rune that holds special meaning for you, or you want to use the power of a specific rune in your daily life, then a necklace, bracelet or brooch bearing that rune might be just the thing for you. Even if you don't work with metal, runic jewellery is available from a number of sources.

Although I have never done it, I have even heard of people baking a set of runes, using a flour, salt and water mixture. If you cannot make your permanent set straight away, this might be a way to create an interim set of runes until you can find that perfect branch, antler or pile of stones.

As long as the materials you use are natural and you keep the dimensions uniform and suitable for your hands, you can allow your own imagination to be your ultimate guide. Anything you craft from nature's bounty can, with symbols applied, become your source for runic divination.

WORKING WITH RUNES

THE RUNE POUCH

Now that you have your runes, you will need a pouch in which to keep them. This will keep your runes together, so that you don't lose any. It also serves as a possible means for drawing runes when you are doing a reading.

The pouch should be large enough to hold the rune stones comfortably. You need to be able to put your hand in and pull out a rune with ease. But keep the pouch small enough so that you won't be able to see which runes your hand is choosing. The pouch can be made of silk, satin, leather, cotton or any other natural material.

Choose a colour that you personally respond to or is symbolic for you. Blue affects me more than any other colour, so my preference is for a rich, deep blue. You can also match the colour of the runic symbols if you painted your rune stones.

The top of the pouch should have a drawstring, so you can close it when your runes are not in use. If you are handy with a needle and thread, you can make your own pouch. If not, you can buy one.

Unlike your runes, the pouch does not carry any special 'magic' if home made and I am not just saying that because I can't sew a stitch. However, making anything by hand means it is special, simply because it is your skill that brought it into being.

BONDING WITH YOUR RUNES

This may sound strange, but over time you will build a bond between yourself and your runes. They are yours and no one else's. Therefore, you should not let others touch them. You want your energy in the stones, not that of a stranger.

If you carry your runes about with you, this bond will grow stronger more quickly. Putting the pouch in a pocket or tying it onto your belt will give you a sense of the runes' presence and will aid in imprinting your energy on the stones.

You don't have to go crazy, like wearing them on your wedding day or to that big job interview. As with all things, use your better judgement. But don't dismiss the idea that there is more to the runes than symbols on wood, bone, stone or clay. The more respect you give the runes, the more guidance they will give back to you.

DRAWING AND CASTING

When you are ready to do a reading, find a quiet spot so that you can concentrate without interruption. Spread your rune cloth (a square of white or black silk is an excellent choice) so that your runes are kept clean and will show up clearly. Hold your rune pouch in your hands and take three deep breaths, in through the nose and out through the mouth. This will help to 'centre' you and your breath will infuse the space around you with your essence. If you are comfortable doing so, say a brief prayer asking for guidance and the wisdom to understand the messages you will receive.

It is traditional to ask the runes a question. The question can be specific or general, but be careful in your wording. If the question is not exactly that for which you seek answers, you may get a response that does not make sense, until you realize that your question was vague or wrongly worded. It is also important to be honest about your question. Be sure you ask about what is really on your mind, or you could send two messages – one that you ask openly and one that is spoken by your secret voice.

When you know what you want to ask, hold your rune pouch next to your heart and concentrate on the question. You are asking for guidance from an oracle, so focus your mental energy. When you feel it is time, you can begin to draw or cast your runes.

What is the difference between drawing and casting? When you draw a rune, you are picking it out of the group. To use this method, you can keep the runes in your pouch. Shake the pouch to shuffle the stones, while thinking about the question you want to ask. When you feel they are sufficiently shuffled, reach blindly into the pouch and pick out a rune. You can take whichever rune you touch first, or you can sift them all through your fingers, until one just seems to 'stick' or makes its presence felt. Often, one stone in particular 'feels' right. It may seem to stick to your fingers or palm while others flow freely through; or it may feel a little hotter, or have more latent energy. The important thing is to trust yourself. Regardless of how subtle the message, allow one rune to be your choice. As long as you don't cheat by looking, you won't get it wrong.

Casting involves 'throwing' the runes. I don't mean whipping them across the room; it is more like spilling them from the pouch or gently tossing them onto your rune cloth. When they are all there, turn them face down and gently mix or shuffle them so that you no longer know which is which. This method does not work well if your rune stones are irregularly shaped or easily recognizable. It is important that you don't impose your will on the stones, trying to 'pick the good ones' or the ones you *think* you should get.

When the stones are thoroughly shuffled, blindly choose the runes for your reading. You can do this by using your intuition. Hover the palm of your hand over the stones, or touch each one on the back, waiting until you feel the energy or

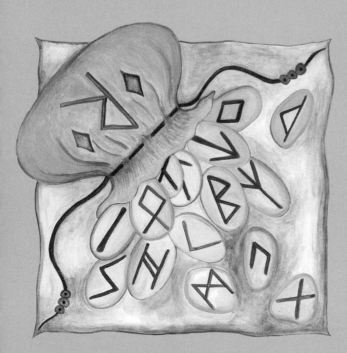

heat mentioned earlier. If you have difficulty 'feeling' the stones, you can pull in a pattern, like picking the stones that are furthest to the left or right, or one from each corner. The more you experiment, the more you will find a method that suits you, whether it is drawing, casting, feeling for energy or developing a pattern.

If you are doing a reading for someone other than yourself, you can use the same methods, but be sure to keep a strong focus on the questioner, so that your own energy does not interfere. Some people wonder if it will hurt their relationship with their runes if they use their energy to answer the questions of another person. I feel that helping someone else can only strengthen your relationship with the runes. As long as it is positive energy being brought to bear – a genuine wish to help another human being – then there is nothing to cause hurt. However, if you are trying to harm someone, then you are doing more to harm yourself than others.

LAYOUTS

You have your stones spread out and ready to choose, or your hand is in the bag. Now what? In the third part of this book, you will find a large section on layouts and spreads, with a focus on sample questions and readings. Unless you are drawing a single stone, you will be placing the runes in a preset pattern. This means that not only do the different runes have meanings, but the positions in which they land also have a significance. There are even associations between the runes themselves: one rune can influence another if they are both in the layout, especially if they are close to each other.

So, when you draw your stones, it is important to think about which position on the layout you are drawing. As you pick each stone, place it on the cloth, still upside down, in the position it will occupy in the layout. When you have drawn all the stones, you can turn them over to see what you have.

MEANINGS OF THE RUNES

In the second part of this book, you will find the meanings of each of the 24 runes of the Elder Futhark and the blank rune. When you first begin working with the runes, you will probably have to refer to those pages quite often. The more you learn, however, the more you will get a sense of the various meanings. Soon you will begin to bring your own interpretations to them as well.

Don't feel bad if at first the names of the runes sound strange, if you can't tell some of them apart or if the meanings don't pop into your head as soon as you see the symbols. Like any new skill, reading the runes takes time, patience and practice.

KEEPING A RUNE JOURNAL

One of the more fascinating aspects of reading runes is what you will bring to them. The more you work with them, the more you will have flashes of insight, glimpses of meanings and thoughts that stretch beyond what you will read in this or any other rune book. These will help you to forge a personal relationship with the runes.

It is important not to allow these flashes and glimpses to disappear. This is why a rune journal is an essential tool. You can set up your journal in any way that pleases you, but one necessary component is a listing of the runes, with plenty of room to fill in your own thoughts, observations and insights about each symbol. Give yourself plenty of room to write, and allow yourself to record any observation, regardless of whether or not you think it has deep meaning or true significance. Sometimes, the biggest insights begin with the smallest of thoughts.

Writing about each of the runes separately will also help you familiarize yourself with them. The more you observe and contemplate the individual runes, the better sense you will get of their meaning in your life.

In another part of your journal, you can record the readings you have done for yourself or others, and what your interpretations were. This can be an invaluable resource not only for gleaning past insights, but also for tracking the patterns of your life. You can also get a sense of which runes you draw more often, which ones rarely show up, and so on.

Drawing a morning rune is another wonderful way to get acquainted with your runes, track your progress and document yet more of your insights into their meanings. Having a set number of questions aids this process. For example, once you have your morning rune, you can look for its shape throughout your day. Ask yourself 'Did this rune make a difference in how I made decisions today?' or 'Which aspect of the rune did I feel most strongly today?' The questions you ask are limited only by your own imagination. Try to make them universal. If they are too specific, they might not be relevant to every day or every rune. With general questions, the answers will come, especially if you have carried your daily rune in your mind throughout the day.

Anything that involves your relationship with the oracle can go in your rune journal. You can save some pages for personal thoughts and observations that are based, not on a single rune, but rather on the impact they have had on your life. The more information and insights you write down, the more material you will have as you move from the introductory phases of discovery to greater understanding of the runes and their role in your world.

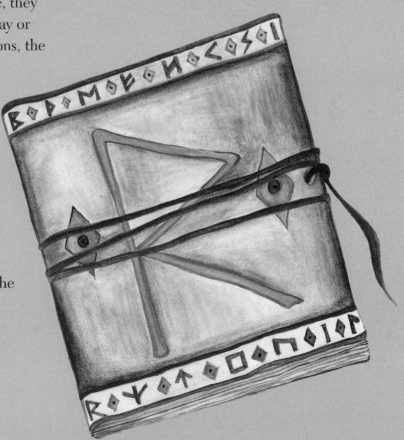

READING RUNES

Welcome to the main event: the runes themselves, what they stand for and

guidance on how to interpret them. The pages are colour-coded to make

each rune easier to find when you do a reading.

You will notice that some runes have both an upright and a reversed interpretation. If you draw a reversed stone, it can help to understand its message if you read both the upright and reversed interpretations of the rune, especially if it notes that these meanings are similar.

As you begin to familiarize yourself with the various runes and their meanings, you will see several themes beginning to take shape. Some runes deal with health and some with romance. There are runes of delay and runes of prosperity. It helps if you become familiar with some of these groupings, because all the runes in a spread interact with and affect each other. A reading full of health runes tends to send a clear message, even if a couple of the individual stones are not from that group.

RUNES AS 'GUIDES'

One of the primary things to remember is that runes are an oracle, not a fortune-teller. They are not trying to 'predict' some fated future that cannot be changed.

Instead, they point out potential areas for you to examine in your life. If you ask about your finances and get several reversed prosperity runes, look at the message they are trying to send. It is not 'you will die poor'. More likely they will point to something in your life that, if changed, will open you to what you seek.

You can think of the runes as guides, showing you a possible path towards your desires. It is important to look inwards when doing a reading, because you will know far better than anyone else what message is being sent.

FINDING THE MESSAGE

Another thing to remember is that not every sentence written about a rune is going to apply in each reading. It is up to you to find the message within the interpretation. Sometimes you will have drawn a rune for one, specific reason, buried among things that don't apply to your situation. Don't let this frustrate you. In subsequent readings, those other messages may apply.

Each runecast is different. Each has its own message to impart. It is up to you to find it. If this sounds difficult, it is not. I have found it remarkably easy to find those things that resonate within me, as have all the people for whom I have done personal readings. This individuality is part of the magic of the rune stones.

A NOTE ABOUT WYRD

Wyrd is a blank rune that was added in modern times. Some people dislike its inclusion in any rune text. I have included it because I want you to have a choice. I see no reason to impose my will on your rune reading. If you don't like it, then pretend it is not there. If you do, then it is available to you.

FEHU

REVERSED

Drawing Fehu in the reversed position could point to a financial loss if care is not taken. Delays, obstacles and frustration could be your only reward. You might want to re-evaluate your current plans. Sometimes it is better to admit to a mistake, take your losses and move on to another, safer project. Otherwise, you are going to find you have chosen a difficult and financially threatening path.

If your overall reading is a negative one, the reversing of Fehu is a strong warning to abandon risky plans now, before you lose all that you have worked for. However, if your overall reading is a positive one, the reversing of Fehu deals more with obstacles and delays rather than with loss and failure.

Fehu can also apply to emotional issues. If you are worried about a relationship, a reversed Fehu tells you that the timing may not be right. Don't let the arguments, doubts and suspicions tear you apart. Look for the deeper meaning and anticipate problems before they arise. Don't blow up small incidents out of proportion. This could be a temporary situation. A strong relationship takes a great deal of work. Give it time, patience and care, and it will become clear what you can do.

Whether it is love or wealth, a reversed Fehu is telling you that care must be taken. Be alert to situations or relationships that appear good today, but may bring problems in the future.

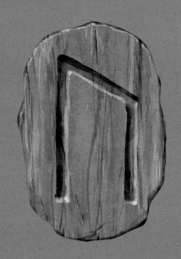

URUZ

UPRIGHT

SYMBOL OF STRENGTH AND CHANGE

ORIGIN OF THE WORD: AUROCHS

Uruz is the name the northern Europeans gave to the 'aurochs', a wild and ferocious breed of ox. Young boys were considered men only after they had participated in an aurochs' kill. It was a sign of virility and a coming of age. Uruz is a powerful symbol of strength and change.

TRANSITIONS

Often a transitional rune, Uruz could indicate an exciting opportunity or new responsibility. This change could include sacrifice. There are times when, in order to advance, we must discard those things we no longer need. What once was good may now be ending. This is not a time for sentimentality. What you gain will far outweigh what you need to lose. You have the power within you to meet any challenge and overcome it. Yes, change can be frightening (it is only natural to fear what you do not know), but have faith in yourself and courage will replace the fear.

PROSPERITY

In business, Uruz often indicates a step up. You will have to work hard and pay attention to details as well as the big picture. This will be noticed by those in a position to help you and could lead to a promotion or even a new career. You have all the strength, vitality and mental prowess necessary to handle these new responsibilities. If the rest of your reading is positive, you have an excellent chance to be successful in whatever you choose at this time.

HEALTH

Uruz is also a symbol of vigorous health. It shows you have recuperative strength and the power to resist diseases. If you are currently ill, Uruz indicates a swift return to good health. You have an enviable amount of stamina and will not let ill health take hold of you. If you are a woman, Uruz points to a man in your life whose sexual urges and passion for you are heightened. If you are a man, Uruz indicates that your sexual urges and passions are at their peak.

RELATIONSHIPS

Drawing an upright Uruz indicates that this is an excellent time to settle any disputes you may be involved in. In this time of exceptional strength and openness to change, you are especially capable of tackling the disagreements that may have been clinging to you and keeping you from meeting your full potential.

However, just because you have strength does not mean you should attack life with arrogance. The very strong can afford to be humble. They have no need to constantly prove their worth. A dash of humility in all your dealings, whether business, romantic or personal, will take you much farther than pure, aggressive bull-headedness.

Drawing an upright Uruz is a wonderful indication that you are capable of playing whatever hand life deals you. Use that strength wisely and generously.

URUZ

REVERSED

Uruz reversed portends opportunities that may be missed due to lack of self-esteem. You should not let an opportunity go by where you can show the world what makes you special. It takes strength to meet a challenge and overcome it. It is only natural to fear what you do not know, but have faith in yourself and you will find that courage replaces the fear.

Because Uruz is a stone of strength, it implies weakness when reversed. This takes the form of weak willpower. You may have found yourself being easily swayed lately. Those people around you who exert their own personalities may find it easy to talk you into all manner of things. It is time for you to take control of your life. You are the captain of your destiny and things never work out if you ignore your instincts. If you have Wunjo or Gebo in your reading, it implies that your partner, whether romantic or business, is the one exerting this influence. You may perceive them as too strong for you and therefore let them have their way.

In health matters, Uruz reversed points to low vitality, which can lead to health problems or illness. Attitude has a great impact on health. If you think positively and fight against whatever ails you, you could be taking a giant step forward. Stress reduction is also a key factor. Now is the time for you to draw on your inner strength and maintain a positive outlook.

THURISAZ

UPRIGHT

SYMBOL OF PROTECTION AND LUCK

ORIGIN OF THE WORD: GIANT, THORN, THE GOD THOR

Thurisaz is associated with the Norse god Thor and his magical hammer, Mjollnir. When the runic alphabet was introduced in ancient England, they renamed it 'Thorn' because the picture on the rune resembled one. Thor and a thorn both bring images of protection.

LUCK

Thurisaz is also associated with luck. This is the kind of luck we would all like to have. Sometimes it can be from a friend or lover, but more often it is from an unknown and unexpected source. It is like being in the right place at the right time. If you have Algiz or Eihwaz in your reading, your luck will be especially good.

Unfortunately, it can also mean your current run of good luck is about to end, especially if your runecast is negative. This does not have to happen. Thurisaz is a warning to be more careful. You may need to think about what you are doing. Don't recklessly jump into something that needs more thought. Be aware that it could be your own stubbornness that causes problems. If this is the case, try to ease yourself away from an 'I'm right, you're wrong' attitude. Keep an open mind, and you will find a solution.

OBSTACLES

A thorn can also be an obstacle or an obstruction. This is an excellent time to do some hard thinking, to see if you are building barriers in your life. Use your courage and humility to overcome them.

If delay runes such as Isa, Nauthiz or Hagalaz are present, Thurisaz is a warning that you may want to postpone any project that you were thinking about starting. Timing can be extremely important in any new venture, so this is a strong hint to look at your timetable so that you can choose a more auspicious starting date.

Coupled with Ansuz, Jera or Mannaz, Thurisaz takes on an additional meaning. If for some reason you are being pushed into making a decision, seek professional help from someone like a lawyer, a consultant or a doctor. You need to talk to a person who is not as close to the problem or has more expertise than you. Listen carefully to the advice and you will have far more information for making your final decision.

PROTECTION

Thurisaz is also a stone of protection. Because it is so closely associated with luck, however, it is the kind of protection luck provides. If, for instance, you owned an expensive car (which would be lucky indeed) and someone tried to steal it, it would be terrible. But say a neighbour interrupted the thief, the car alarm scared them off or they simply could not get the ignition to work, then through a lucky break you would still have your car. It was protected by luck. This is the kind of protection Thurisaz gives you.

THURISAZ

REVERSED

Thurisaz means almost the same thing when reversed as it does upright (not that you will want to hear that). It is difficult to get someone who drew a reversed Thurisaz to listen to advice. Unfortunately, the consequences of following only your ideas, seeing only your side of things and blindly forging ahead are now worse than ever.

A reversed Thurisaz can mean that someone subordinate to you, someone you see as weaker, is causing trouble. You are seeing them as some sort of threat. This does not just apply to business, it can be found anywhere in your life. It can also be your fear that a protégé of yours is going to fail and therefore make you look bad. If

Kenaz is in the reversed position in your reading, it is a signal that this person is about to come forward. It also indicates that you fear this person will outdo you in some way.

Your luck is running out fast, and now more than ever you need to use caution. A quick decision now is almost guaranteed to be a bad one because it is coming from weakness. It is easy to deceive yourself about your motives. This internal blindness will only worsen a situation that is already getting bad. Since you cannot rely on luck – for it is likely to be bad luck – deliberate thinking is your best weapon against further problems.

ANSUZ

UPRIGHT

SYMBOL OF THE SPOKEN WORD, WISDOM AND ADVICE

ORIGIN OF THE WORD: MOUTH

Ansuz is associated with the spoken word. Since the northern Europeans were schooled in the oral tradition (for example, an elder passing on stories to an apprentice) it also means acquired wisdom. The taking of advice is yet another application of Ansuz.

TEST

There are several ways in which these different aspects of Ansuz are seen. For instance, there may be a test coming in the near future. This may be an exam or a job interview, but it does not have to be one of these. It can mean a testing experience. We all learn from what life teaches us and things often feel like a test. Regardless of what it is, you will speak well and be successful, however you are tested.

ADVICE

Wisdom and advice go hand in hand, making this a very strong message. The spoken word is not just from you, but from others around you. It could be a parent, teacher, doctor, lawyer – anyone who is more learned than you in the subject in question. Take this wiser person's advice, because Ansuz is telling you that it will be open, honest and very helpful. Some liken Ansuz to a gift, and that gift is often knowledge. Pay close attention when you are with those who are older and wiser, for they may impart the key that unlocks a knotty situation in your life.

There may be travel coming up in the near future. If you are travelling, it will possibly be a trip to visit a friend or relative who can advise and instruct you. More likely, this person will be visiting you.

The other stones in your reading may indicate who it is that will be visiting and advising. If Berkana is present, it will most likely be a close relative, such as a parent, sibling or child. Othala indicates an older relative – a grandparent, perhaps. If you have drawn Jera, it points to someone official, such as a lawyer.

APPRENTICESHIP

Another aspect of Ansuz is apprenticeship. You may have a chance to learn a new trade. It could even be an opportunity, adventure or problem that you have never had to deal with before. Happily, Ansuz tells you that there is someone nearby who is willing to help and guide you through it. They will be patient, understanding and knowledgeable. The best move you could possibly make is to listen carefully to their advice and counsel.

RELEASE

Finally, Ansuz is a rune of release. If you carry the burden of fear or anxiety, now is the time to let it go. Fear can influence your decisions to your detriment. Anxiety can colour your emotional world with a broad brush. When you ask yourself how these fears are serving you, you will realize that they are stifling your voice. Divest yourself and your voice of these imagined chains and experience the sublime reward of freedom.

ANSUZ
REVERSED

A reversed Ansuz is a warning that someone is giving you bad advice. It may be a parent or a boss, or anyone in a position higher than you. Be especially wary if you hear something important relating to your current circumstances. Get a second opinion and consider all advice with some suspicion. These same people may be trying to interfere with your current plans. You may be feeling frustrated and confused because communication has broken down and you don't understand something that once seemed simple.

Reversed, Ansuz points to a web of lies and deceit. Be aware of possible untruths. You might find unwelcome duties, as well. Elderly relatives can be a burden because of illness or age. They may interfere with your plans, but are not to blame. This innocent yet vexing stumbling block to your own desires is yet another challenge.

The problem could also lie within you. It is important that you learn from life's lessons. Adversity can be the greatest teacher of all. Don't fight, complain and moan about your fate, and then continue to make the same mistakes. Your tendency may be to learn, yet never use or share your knowledge. Find a constructive purpose for your wisdom and you will know a greater joy than you will ever get from information.

A reversed Ansuz is a signpost. Life is the one exam we all must take and only by learning can we hope to pass this test.

RAIDHO

UPRIGHT

SYMBOL OF JOURNEYS, TRAVEL AND MOVEMENT
ORIGIN OF THE WORD: RIDING

Raidho is often called 'wagon' or 'cartwheel'. Because of these associations, Raidho is the travelling rune or the symbol of journeys. In a broader context, it means movement of any kind.

TRAVEL

The travelling might be a physical journey. This will probably be a pleasure trip, not for business or through necessity. It might mean a family vacation or a holiday from work. If you are planning a trip, an upright Raidho is wonderful news. Your voyage will be pleasant and trouble-free and you will have excellent company to share it with.

It can also mean a journey of the spirit. Are you travelling the correct path through life? There is an aspect of change to Raidho, especially when referring to a spiritual journey. Don't be surprised if you find yourself veering in a new direction when you examine your life's goals. You may even retain the same goals, but will decide to travel on a different path to attain them. A deep look inside yourself can be frightening, but the timing is right for both the introspection and change.

RELATIONSHIPS

Logic and clear thinking will be your assets in the next couple of months, so it is a good time for serious discussions and important negotiations. If you are currently having trouble coming to an agreement with someone, there is a viable compromise available and together you will reach it.

Messages often take their own journey. In the days of the Vikings, they were sent by runners carrying sticks covered in runes or by repeating a message orally. An upright Raidho can mean some sort of message by letter, email or telephone. This message is often unexpected or gives unexpected news. Get ready to take advantage of this surprising development.

If your reading is primarily negative, be extra careful when listening to the advice and counsel of others. The spoken word can be unreliable. If you have a reversed Perthro, there could be a broken promise. A reversed Algiz means someone may be trying to take advantage of you.

PROSPERITY

In most situations, an upright Raidho tells you that you are in an excellent position. Your mind is sharp, your bargaining skills high and your business sense honed. If you are contemplating some sort of action, be it in business or otherwise, now is the time to act. But be aware that good sense does not necessarily include blind trust. Read the small print in contracts and don't trust everything you hear. People may take advantage of your willingness to bargain.

All in all, an upright Raidho is an excellent sign that things are going your way.

RAIDHO
REVERSED

A reversed Raidho warns of travel problems. You may be forced to take a trip you weren't planning. It could come at a bad time or be caused by unfortunate circumstances. A friend or relative might be sick or in trouble, and you have to drop everything to go to their side. Alternatively, it can mean that another person may visit you at a most inconvenient moment.

If you are planning a trip, a reversed Raidho can point to the kind of journey only a stand-up comedian would joke about. You could lose your luggage, suffer delays, miss connections, have mechanical problems and even have a minor accident.

Unfortunately, Raidho in the reversed position also says that those plans and schemes you have been working on will somehow get messed up. This is therefore not the time to conduct a serious negotiation or implement an important plan, because a monkey wrench could be thrown into the middle of it all and things could go awry. If you are aware of this possibility when you are going into the situation, then you may be able to minimize the damage. Your usually sharp mind is a little dulled right now, so try to give extra effort and thought to all of your current projects.

Lastly, be conscious of the emotional states of those around you. Tempers are going to be on edge and it is up to you to display as much patience and humour as possible to defray some of the tension.

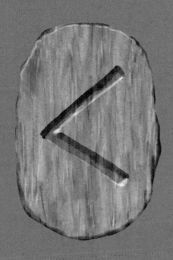

KENAZ

UPRIGHT

SYMBOL OF HEALTH, GIFTS AND CREATIVITY

ORIGIN OF THE WORD: TORCH

A torch is a form of controlled fire. Like the warm, cosy blazes in a fireplace or the soft, comforting glow of the modern electric light, the ancients took the savage power of fire and tamed it for their own uses. Kenaz symbolizes the strength, energy and power of fire, as well as the protection it gives from predators in the night.

HEALTH

An upright Kenaz is a wonderful omen. It signifies excellent health and powers of recuperation. It is the strength of your positive attitude that most aids your physical wellbeing. Kenaz also indicates a time of positive thought. Your normal worries will lessen and the few problems that do occur will be easily solved.

RELATIONSHIPS

An upright Kenaz also represents the relationship between two people and the giving of a gift. Although this is often a romantic or sexual relationship, it does not have to be. Because Kenaz represents male energy, it will be the man giving the gift and the female receiving. In a business relationship, the giver would be the boss, in families, the parent. Think about the question you

GEBO

SYMBOL OF PARTNERSHIPS, LOVE AND GIFTS

ORIGIN OF THE WORD: GIFT

Gebo probably stems from gifts offered to, or by, the gods. In early Germanic literature, there are many references to chieftains giving gifts to trusted followers. Because Gebo is a sign in which two strong lines support each other, it also stands for partnerships (as in love or business). There is no reversed meaning to Gebo, so it is a positive sign.

A LOVING KISS

Gebo is the only rune that is still commonly used in today's culture. Every time you put an 'X' at the bottom of a letter to symbolize a kiss (romantic partnership), you are using the rune Gebo.

RELATIONSHIPS

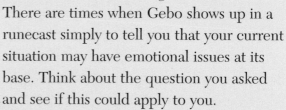

Partnerships play a big role in a runecast including Gebo. Although it can be any kind of partnership, it often heralds a new twist in a romantic relationship. This could be anything from a stronger sense of commitment to a marriage. There are times when Gebo shows up in a runecast simply to tell you that your current situation may have emotional issues at its base. Think about the question you asked and see if this could apply to you.

It might also be a business partnership. The mutual support you will give each other will be very important to both of you, so treat this relationship with the respect and honour it deserves. Your success will be greater in tandem than individually.

PROSPERITY

Whatever the gift, it will be appreciated. Gebo's gift usually comes at a most fortunate time. For example, it might be money from an unexpected source just when you need it most, or something that is exactly what you want. It can also be an emotional gift, given to you with love.

Most likely, the gift will come with an obligation of a return, like bartering. Because of this, be aware of your part of the bargain, for you must be willing to part with something of equal value in return. The good news is that this exchange will benefit both of you, because each of you will gain far more than you will lose. For example, if someone had two horses and someone else had two carts, an exchange would give each a horse and cart, which would benefit them both.

WISDOM

The gift may also come in the form of wisdom. According to the Norse legend, Odin traded one of his eyes in exchange for the gift of wisdom. Although you won't be asked to pay such a high price, you will be obliged to use the wisdom correctly. Don't abuse this gift, because the consequences could be dire.

Gebo itself is a gift in a runecast because it often signifies that your troubles are almost over. Look forward to a break from the stresses of your daily life.

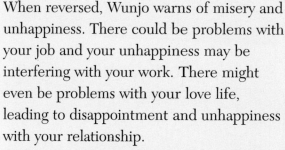

WUNJO

REVERSED

When reversed, Wunjo warns of misery and unhappiness. There could be problems with your job and your unhappiness may be interfering with your work. There might even be problems with your love life, leading to disappointment and unhappiness with your relationship.

If you are planning to travel, and have Raidho or Ehwaz in your runecast, there might be trouble on the journey and an unsuccessful conclusion.

In love and business, it would be wise to be aware of an outsider who may cause trouble. This person could try to create delays or instigate friction between you and your partner or boss. Treachery is a real possibility. It will be difficult to guard against a clandestine opponent, but if you and your partner or boss discuss and understand the dangers, you will be that much closer to defeating the interloper.

The overriding message of Wunjo reversed is one of caution. If an important trip, decision or event is at hand, delay it if you can. The number six is closely related to Wunjo; so, for a more specific guideline, the delay should be six days, six weeks or six months.

Remember that everything negative can be seen as a test or an opportunity to learn. Be sincere and flexible in your dealings with others. You have a chance to turn things around because you are aware of the dangers. Drawing a reversed Wunjo means that it is time to meditate and prepare for life's battles.

HAGALAZ

**SYMBOL OF DAMAGING NATURAL
FORCES, DISRUPTION
ORIGIN OF THE WORD: HAIL**

Every farmer knows that hail's destructive balls of ice can fall mercilessly and unexpectedly from the sky, destroying anything on the ground. Whole fields can be flattened with one hailstorm. Hagalaz represents the uncontrollable outside forces that can sweep into your life, leaving you with a world that is not the same as it was the day before.

DELAY

If you have a generally positive runecast, it may be less of a disruption than an interruption. A small delay may counteract the forces of Hagalaz. If your positive runecast includes delay runes such as Isa, Nauthiz or a reversed Othala, use the breathing space to consider changing those things in your life that are no longer having a positive influence.

Hagalaz has no reversed position, but has many negative connotations. Risks are an everyday part of life, yet drawing this stone

suggests that now is not the time to take risks unduly. In business, romance and travel, there is an element of unknown consequence waiting to strike if you are too bold or daring.

RISK

If your reading includes Fehu or Jera, you may need to work harder than you thought, but eventually you will succeed. The rune Perthro in conjunction with Hagalaz shows that you may get a monetary bonus or win the lottery. If you have drawn the reverses of Jera, Fehu or Perthro, avoid all risky undertakings at this time. Stick to things that are safe and stable, as opposed to risky and daring.

DISRUPTION

Remember that disruptive events don't have to be negative. The birth of a child is very disruptive, yet is a time of supreme joy. Often it is best to look at the force that is causing change and try to discern a way of turning it to your advantage. Every negative can turn to a positive if you can see the possibilities instead of the problems.

Runes of creativity, such as Kenaz or Tiwaz, give a promise of fertility. This is not limited to birth and babies, but includes a burgeoning of the mind, spirit and body. This is also true for fertility runes, such as Berkana, Laguz or Ingwaz. Take advantage of this gift.

Because Hagalaz is a rune of outside forces and disruption, it may be someone unknown to you who is the cause. It won't be a personal vendetta, but more that of an official, government worker or lawyer bearing a message. It is not necessarily bad news, just unexpected. Any problems it causes can be assuaged by relying on your own inner strength.

This is an excellent opportunity to foster inner growth. You create your own life, and outside forces can be seen as internal tests. Use this time to develop your flexibility. Learn to eliminate those things that you cannot control as sources of stress, fear and anxiety. Emulate the grasses that spring back towards the sun when the hailstorm has passed.

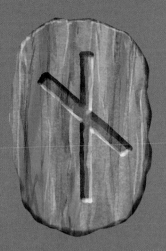

NAUTHIZ

UPRIGHT

SYMBOL OF NEED, NECESSITY AND CONSTRAINT

ORIGIN OF THE WORD: NEED

Nauthiz is sandwiched between the runes that are named after hail and ice. In this position, one can see the reason for it being the rune of need, necessity and constraint. With a delay rune as strong as this, now is not the time to rush headlong into new endeavours.

HEALTH

You may find yourself harassed by delays and constraints, perhaps plagued by ill health. There could even be a chronic health problem. If health is not a problem right now, you should not stretch yourself too much.

An increase in stress can easily lead to illness in your present vulnerable state. Start conserving your energy.

Problems are never fun, but Nauthiz has hope. Things will work out; you will simply have to let time weave its spell. You can't hurry the process.

DELAY

Whenever you pass through a period of your life when you are needy and powerless, the best choice is to take the experience and learn from it. It is this learning period and the lessons you accumulate that will be your strength when faced with problems in the future. You will emerge from this when you face your fears, conserve your energy and learn from mistakes. If you heed this advice, the rewards will be great.

RELATIONSHIPS

'Need' can take many forms. In romantic matters, drawing an upright Nauthiz can mean that the longings of your heart are unanswered. Your partner may be blind to your needs and desires. Perhaps if you explained to your romantic partner the various aspects of the void in your relationship, you could both learn and grow. But be sure that the needs you are addressing are genuine. Minor wants and wishes, when given the strength of true needs, could further damage your relationship. If, however, it is a matter of delays that is bothering you, let them add to the fire of your emotions, using time to strengthen your love.

PROSPERITY

This is also a time to avoid compulsive choices. Think in terms of fulfilling your basic requirements, instead of revelling in luxuries. If you indulge your shallow desires, they may come back to haunt you later. It is also an excellent time to pay off your old debts. This is the perfect opportunity to clear the slate so that you are ready for any new, exciting opportunities that come your way. Without this preparation, you could get caught needing, instead of receiving.

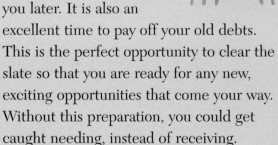

NECESSITY

Another aspect of an upright Nauthiz is necessity, which can arise when need forces you to find a solution. The solution to this necessity could be the breakthrough that alleviates a lot of need. The good news is that it never would have happened had you not found this need inside.

NAUTHIZ

REVERSED

There are times when you make choices against the advice of others and even against your own better judgement. This could have disastrous results. Now is not the time to trample upon others or to go against your own moral code.

Think carefully about the consequences of any action. Don't act on impulse or make snap judgements. If, however, you have already started something, it is not too late. Admit to yourself that you were wrong and concentrate instead on recouping what you can. The consequence of a misguided path is despair. Your self-respect is worth more than money, prestige or sexual fulfilment.

It is even possible that a nefarious scheme you have begun will pay off – in a material sense. But don't expect to be able to sleep at night. It is imperative that you make a sincere effort to right any wrongs, regardless of the price. Otherwise, fate will deliver a severe payback.

If Wyrd is in your runecast, a reversed Nauthiz tells you it is time to own up to your past and start repaying the people you have hurt. If you have drawn Jera, there is trouble with the law ahead if you don't act immediately. In conjunction with Hagalaz, you may be reprimanded by God or nature.

You will become a stronger and more enlightened person if you resist this temptation. Think of this not as 'gloom and doom' but as an opportunity for unparalleled growth.

ISA

SYMBOL OF A FREEZE
ORIGIN OF THE WORD: ICE

Ice is cold and hard, and can be treacherous. Yet it can also have glistening beauty. Ice is a way of preserving things. You freeze food so that you can enjoy later what would once have been thrown away. Isa has no reverse and is a rune of delay. If you put your plans on ice for a time, when the moment is right you can defrost them when they have a greater chance of success.

RELATIONSHIPS

With relationships, whether business, romantic, family or friend, Isa denotes a cooling-down period. Loyalty plays a big role in all these affiliations, and it is this quality that may be in question. Sometimes it is you who has been disloyal, but more often it is another. If the disloyalty is too great, and no amount of delays can calm the situation, then step back and re-evaluate the importance of this person in your life. If the person or relationship is basically good, then fight for it. Let the situation 'cool down' and then show the person that there is fire beneath the ice.

Sometimes we are driven to things we can't help by circumstances beyond our control. However, if your reading is primarily negative, you may be fighting for a lost cause. It is probably time to cut your losses and move on.

PROCRASTINATION

Procrastination may also be a problem for you. If you have been plagued by this common, yet insidious, habit, it is time

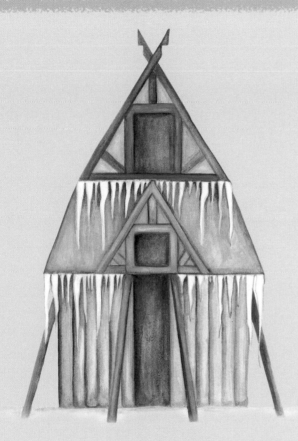

for you to search your soul for the reasons why. There are several causes, but fear is the most likely. During this time of natural delay, face your fear and draw it out into the open. Only by acknowledging and then conquering it can you dispel the fear, and the procrastination it causes.

There is a positive aspect to Isa: the delay gives you time to evaluate and mull over your choices. It is a time for renewal and introspection. If you are faced with a difficult problem, now is the perfect time to sit quietly and work out a solution.

HEALTH

Ice is also water, a necessity of life. When liquid, water is often restless, flowing in streams, raining down from the skies or crashing on shorelines in powerful waves. Freezing gives water a time to rest. To remain healthy and happy, you also need rest. If your life is filled with flowing, crashing downpours of activity, this is the perfect time to escape. Take some time off, go on a holiday or simply take some time to indulge in a relaxing hobby.

PROSPERITY

The freeze applies to goals, business and other plans as well. You may find yourself in a restless game of waiting. With each day that passes, your frustration increases. In this case, a brief delay is all that is necessary. Use the time for preparation and you will be happier for it in the end.

JERA

SYMBOL OF HARVEST, JUSTICE, FULL CYCLE

ORIGIN OF THE WORD: YEAR

A farmer plants his seeds, waters them, tends them, watches over them and nurtures them through the seasons until finally it is time to harvest. The harvest is the reward for his hard work and tender care. Jera symbolizes your reward. It has no reverse position and is generally a very positive sign. It is the culmination of hard work and a reaping of benefits.

JUSTICE

Jera's association with hard work equalling just rewards gives it another connotation – justice. This is often justice in a legal sense and therefore it extends to all legal action, whether it benefits you or not. There could be a court case in your future, but not necessarily. Jera can refer to anything that is legal, including contracts. These might be business contracts, marriage contracts, wills, licences – anything legally binding.

If Ansuz or Mannaz is in your runecast, the pairing with Jera shows that you may be seeking or receiving legal advice in the near future. It could even point to advice from other professionals, such as doctors, stockbrokers or bankers.

PATIENCE

Just as the farmer must wait for the crops to yield their bounty, you must have patience. It can be difficult to work hard without seeing progress, but Jera attests that it will be well worth the wait. Unripe fruit is bitter and unsatisfactory, yet fruit that is allowed to mature fills your mouth with sweetness. Patience and hard work will fill your life with its rewards.

If Hagalaz, Nauthiz or Wyrd has shown up, you may be heading down the wrong path. It is not an indication of wrongdoing so much as misdirection. Your talents lie elsewhere, and it is tempting fate to continue on a road that does not suit you.

TRANSITIONS

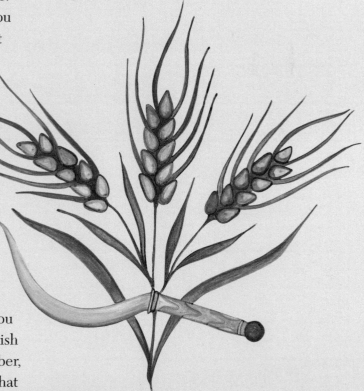

Because Jera means 'year', it also carries the sense of a full cycle. You may have projects that you began last year which are just now coming to fruition. Now is the time to harvest. If you did everything right, and did not try to cheat or hurry the process, then your rewards will be great.

Coming after three powerful delay runes, Jera is the engine that gets things going again. Take advantage of this time of rejuvenation. The earth and the sun provide all the power you need to complete any task. You are refreshed and alive and can accomplish any goal. As if waking from a deep slumber, now is your chance to show the world what you can contribute. Like a farmer who separates the wheat from the chaff, winnow out those things that don't serve you and hold on to the sweet reward of your labour.

Even if your runecast is generally negative, the fact that Jera is there says that, with diligence and effort, you can prevent anything untoward from happening.

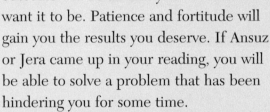

EIHWAZ

SYMBOL OF PROTECTION, FLEXIBILITY AND ENDURANCE

ORIGIN OF THE WORD: YEW

The yew was more than a mere tree to the ancient Nordic people. In their mythology, it was Yggdrasil, the great tree of life. Odin hung upside down from Yggdrasil when he discovered the runes. It was also used to make longbows, a primary weapon of the Nordic people. Because of the yew's legends and uses for defence, Eihwaz stands for protection.

PROSPERITY

Eihwaz has no reverse and is a wonderful, strong rune. If you have set goals, they are within your abilities, talents and energy. You may run into obstacles, delays and twists in your journey, but the outcome will be all that you want it to be. Patience and fortitude will gain you the results you deserve. If Ansuz or Jera came up in your reading, you will be able to solve a problem that has been hindering you for some time.

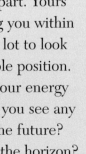

Even when it seems as though you can't possibly dig yourself out of the mess you have made, things can still turn around. Opportunities will present themselves of which you can take advantage. Each of us has unique talents that set us apart. Yours are going to be utilized to bring you within reach of your goals. You have a lot to look forward to and are in an enviable position.

Now is a good time to turn your energy inwards for just a moment. Do you see any problems that might occur in the future? Are there obstacles showing on the horizon? If you take a moment to consider them and think of solutions or detours around them, the obstacles could actually be turned to your advantage.

ENDURANCE

The yew is one of the most long-lived trees. Because of this, Eihwaz also stands for endurance and long life. Like the yew, you will have the endurance to outlast any problems that are currently ongoing. Projects in which you are involved at this time have the potential of long, fruitful lives, once you have overcome the obstacles you currently face. You are in a marathon not a sprint, and eventually you will be triumphant.

FLEXIBILITY

The wood of the yew is extremely strong, yet it is also flexible. This is what made it perfect for making longbows. Now is an excellent time for you to show your own flexibility. Compromise may be the key to the problems you face. When other trees were lashed by storms they would fall, but the yew would bend and sway, its deep roots keeping it strong and healthy. Your own roots are important assets at this time. Look to your family for possible solutions to the troubles you are facing. Another source of roots is your community. Seek out available resources that could hold the answers. Good communication, flexibility and a strong sense of self will carry the day.

PERTHRO

UPRIGHT

SYMBOL OF SECRETS, HIDDEN THINGS, SPECULATION

ORIGIN OF THE WORD: DICE CUP

The original meaning of the word Perthro has been lost in time. Some scholars speculate that it is a dice cup turned on its side. Others feel it is a cauldron on its side. Because of its mysterious origin, Perthro is associated with secrets or things that are hidden.

SECRETS

When you play a game of dice, you don't know which numbers will land upright, but as soon as they are thrown the mystery is solved. With Perthro, secrets that are currently unknown will soon be out in the open. With an upright Perthro, the unknown thing is usually positive. It can be anything from finding a lost possession to the grandest of opportunities.

Secrets are also knowledge that you keep hidden from the world. One of your secrets will soon be out. This could be something you are trying to hide from the world, or simply a piece of information that embarrasses you. It might even be something you don't like discussing or about which you feel shy. Remember, a secret that lies buried beneath layers of guilt can gnaw at you. There are times when the revealing of a secret can be uplifting. There is a feeling of relief and a knowledge that now you can face whatever comes because your soul is clear.

RELATIONSHIPS

The intimate details of your sex life are another 'secret' and therefore under the jurisdiction of Perthro. If you have Kenaz, Tiwaz, Uruz, Gebo, Wunjo, Berkana or Laguz in your reading, you are very sexually compatible with your 'emotional partner'. If you are currently between lovers, there is a good possibility that a new one will soon be entering your life and sexual sparks will fly.

However, with a reversed Uruz, Kenaz or Tiwaz, sex could be the main focus of your current relationship and you might find you have little else. This pairing will flame and turn to ashes if you don't find some other common ground on which to base this partnership. If you are currently between lovers, there is a good possibility that a new one will soon be entering your life. Be aware that the same problem could exist and it might be a relationship based solely on sex.

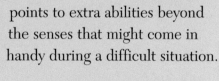

PROSPERITY

Because Perthro has associations with gambling, it indicates that you might be getting some money. It could be a windfall, such as the lottery, or a big win while gambling. The money could also be a gift. If it is, look closely at the giver's motives, because the secrecy of Perthro will apply to them as well. The money might even come in the form of an inheritance.

You might feel a heightened sense of your own intuition. Perthro points to extra abilities beyond the senses that might come in handy during a difficult situation.

PERTHRO

REVERSED

When Perthro is reversed, the secrets it portends are usually dark and buried. They will cause problems when exposed. They may not be your secrets, but their revelation may affect you negatively.

You may also be subject to a financial loss. It is best to avoid lending money. If you do, you may never get it back (even if it is a close friend who borrows it). To get the money returned may be an exhausting struggle and could drain you of much-needed energy. Now is not the time to visit a casino, either. Luck will be against you. Whatever natural intuition you may have will be dampened and hunches may leave you the disappointed party. For a while, things just won't be going your way.

Perthro is also associated with sex. Drawing it reversed shows incompatibility between you and your partner. This is not necessarily a permanent problem, but for a while there may be some missed cues, frustration and a lonely night or two.

If you have Isa or a reversed Uruz, Kenaz or Tiwaz in your runecast, it could be that one partner does not find the other physically attractive any more. Yet the other partner continues to want a sexual relationship. This may be worked out with time and understanding.

Another form of secret is dark magic. However, it is best to avoid the occult right now, because it could lead to difficulties and too much negative attention.

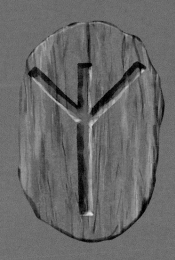

ALGIZ

UPRIGHT

SYMBOL OF PROTECTION, FRIENDSHIP AND DEFENCE

ORIGIN OF THE WORD: PROTECTION/DEFENCE, ELK, SEDGE GRASS

The name of this rune is highly disputed. Some claim it is based on the word for elk and others use the word for sedge grass. The most likely name is Algiz, which means protection and defence. Because the symbol looks somwhat like a person in a stance of prayer, it also means connection to a higher power.

RELATIONSHIPS

An upright Algiz tells you that there is something new and exciting coming into your life. It can be in any form. It could be a new business opportunity, tickets to a show that you thought were unobtainable, a spontaneous holiday, or a new and exciting friend. The only limits are those of your imagination. In fact, this will come about because something in you will react to a situation from your gut, as opposed to your head. You might take a

chance on something, feel an instant bond with someone, or just get an intuition that a choice is the right one. Go with this feeling, for the rewards will be wonderful. Algiz is considered a 'friendship' rune, so be especially on the lookout for a new person in your life. He or she will have a positive influence on you.

PROSPERITY

One of the reasons why it is advisable to take a risk at this time is because of the strong protective influence of Algiz. Whatever choices you make have a good possibility of working out. With a little attentiveness, problems can be avoided. You have as much inner strength as you allow yourself to have. Let the limit go up a few notches because the risks are lessened. After all, your inner voice is always worth listening to, and especially now that its abilities are heightened. If it warns you, listen. If it teases you into new experiences, embrace them. Intuition and conviction are all that you will need.

SPIRITUALITY

Because it connects you to a higher power, Algiz tells you it is a time to honour your own spiritual choice. Whether through prayer, meditation or other practices, show your gratitude for the gifts you have been given, and for the people in your life.

An upright Algiz portends many good things. These joys come not only from the outside (friends, opportunities and so on), but also from inside you. There is no reason not to feel your full potential.

ALGIZ
REVERSED

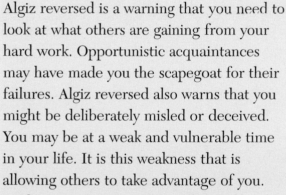

Algiz reversed is a warning that you need to look at what others are gaining from your hard work. Opportunistic acquaintances may have made you the scapegoat for their failures. Algiz reversed also warns that you might be deliberately misled or deceived. You may be at a weak and vulnerable time in your life. It is this weakness that is allowing others to take advantage of you.

If you are starting a new relationship, whether business or romantic, be aware that you are not at your best. Your judgement may be clouded. Look critically at what others want from you. Now would be a good time to review the actions of your partner. If you discover dishonesty, then determine what your partner wants. This knowledge can work to your advantage. Whether or not you choose a confrontation, at least you will not be blindly trusting.

Algiz reversed also functions as a mirror. You may find that you are the cause of your own problems. Are you trying to get something for nothing? If it looks too good to be true, it probably is.

Letting others find your answers for you rarely works, because you can end up being cheated. Awareness of yourself, your potential and the people in your life is one way to gain control. You can lose this control if you are taken in by glib strangers. Pay close attention to what is *really* happening. Only when you are aware of problems can you create solutions.

SOWILO

SYMBOL OF VICTORY, ENERGY AND HEALTH

ORIGIN OF THE WORD: SUN

To the ancients, the sun was considered a beacon of warmth, health and fruitfulness. Their mythology had many examples of gods whose associations were with the sun. Because the sun could melt the frosts, feed the crops and banish darkness, it also became a symbol of victory. Sowilo cannot be reversed and is often a very positive sign that your goals are within reach.

STRESS

Although this is a time of great personal power, there may be an unpleasant by-product – stress. Remember to take care of yourself. Don't lose your perspective. You must do something to relieve the stress. You might want to spend a little time in the sun and relax. It is an excellent source of strength.

If you drew Raidho, Wunjo, Othala, Fehu or Nauthiz, the indications are that you are working too hard. It is not so much that you need to slow down (you probably would find that more stressful than working at your normal pace). It is more that you should channel some of your prodigious energy into some entertaining pursuits. Do something to feed your soul as well as your pocket. Sometimes a little perspective is all that is necessary to melt away the stress.

If your general runecast is negative, you might be worrying about problems without thinking ahead to solutions.

CONTROL

You may feel frustrated when things are out of control. If you are a controlling person whose anxiety level skyrockets, then relax.

beyond your control. If you relax and study the situation, a solution will present itself, especially with the power of Sowilo behind you.

HEALTH

There is excellent and robust health associated with Sowilo. If you have been ill in the past, you may now have the strength and vitality to fight your way back to health. If you drew Kenaz or Tiwaz, you have a keen ability to fight illness. The 'life force' is strong within you. Gebo or Dagaz indicate that you have a marvellous unity between your mind and body. The warmth of Sowilo surrounds you. You are in the enviable position of seeing attainable goals. Here's to your victory!

Deal with what you can, and forget about the rest until a solution presents itself. Accept the lack of control and move on. A reading with Nauthiz, Wyrd, Hagalaz, Isa or Thurisaz compounds this. We are all the centre of our own personal solar system, but you may be pushing this to the extreme. It does not help to let anxiety take over if you run into circumstances that are

TIWAZ

UPRIGHT

SYMBOL OF VICTORY, THE FIGHTING SPIRIT, LAW AND ORDER

ORIGIN OF THE WORD: THE GOD TYR (TIW), SPEAR

Vikings would charge into battle with the rune Tiwaz etched on their helmets and swords. Tyr (or Tiw) was the god of war. The primary meaning of Tiwaz is victory.

PROSPERITY

An upright Tiwaz is so powerful and positive that it carries extra weight in a runecast. Tiwaz, the warrior's symbol, denotes a just cause and a fighter's spirit. It often assures a successful outcome, be it in love, business, health or life in general. You will be challenged, but you have the strength and ability to prevail.

Fighting and victory imply that there is something of value to be gained. The prize will be yours but, more importantly, you will gain the inner pride of knowing success by your own hand. The strength of Tiwaz is really *your* strength and good character. Value that part of yourself.

Tiwaz gives you the energy and inner fortitude necessary to be a champion of those issues you believe in the most. They could be anything, but you will most likely be on the side of the underdog. It might appear to be quixotic, but you will probably succeed despite long odds.

If you have Fehu, Uruz or Sowilo in your reading, the news gets even better. These strong runes combine to make you almost unbeatable. You will go from project to project, gaining allies, character and power.

RELATIONSHIPS

You may be finding a new lover, companion or even spouse. If you are already in love, then your current relationship will deepen and grow.

If you are male, Tiwaz represents you in questions of sex and relationships. In your love life there will be passion, tenderness, joy, excitement and sexual compatibility.

If you are a woman, it represents the man in your life. If there is no man at this time, then be observant, because one is probably on the way. Wunjo, combined with an upright Tiwaz, points to a relationship that has the strength and emotional commitment that will lead to 'happily ever after'. However, if Perthro is showing, the relationship is primarily a sexual one and has little depth.

If you are a woman, a man may assist in your battles. He will be an essential element in your victory. If you have drawn Laguz, you will be the one who does most of the fighting.

If you have a very negative reading, even an upright Tiwaz cannot balance it out. However, remember that abandoning a losing cause carries no shame.

HEALTH

Finally, an upright Tiwaz is a sign of good health. The fighting spirit persists, for you will probably be able to recover quickly from any illness, surgery or disease. After all, there are so many battles left for you to win.

TIWAZ

REVERSED

Do you feel lethargic? Have you lost faith in yourself? To be a winner, you must believe that you are brimming with undiscovered potential. Don't let the apathy and drudgery of a reversed Tiwaz define you. Fight your negative feelings, think positive, and you will be surprised how quickly things change.

You might feel as though your creative juices are not flowing, that you are unfocused and prone to self-pity. This is temporary. Look for the positives in your life and, most importantly, work to regain focus.

If you are a man, or a woman who also drew Laguz, you are prone to taking the easy, less fulfilling way and not fighting for what you deserve. Remember that life does not owe you anything. True happiness comes from the things you work to get and fight to keep. Don't lose the battle before it has even begun.

In romance, a reversed Tiwaz warns of obstacles in your relationship. You say one thing, and your partner another. Listen closely, however, because sometimes you are both making the same statement but using different words. If the relationship is worth saving, it may be up to you to call a truce. But be careful, because a complete confession of your inner heart may be too overwhelming. Reveal your feelings to your partner gradually, so as not to strain the relationship. Blurting out the entire truth will leave your partner either powerless or with fresh ammunition. Work together and love can be reborn.

BERKANA

UPRIGHT

SYMBOL OF FERTILITY AND FAMILY
ORIGIN OF THE WORD: BIRCH TWIG

The birch tree played a key role in ancient fertility rites. Berkana represents you as a twig on your family tree. You are independent of and yet connected to your family. In fact, Berkana is the rune of family and fertility. It is both stability and growth. It stands alone yet is nourished by nature. Motherhood and nurturing form another aspect of Berkana.

TRANSITIONS

Having drawn Berkana, there may be a forthcoming event that includes your family. This is usually a traditional gathering that often indicates a rite of passage, such as the birth of a child, a christening, a coming-of-age party, a wedding, a reunion, a graduation, an anniversary or a retirement. This will be a warm and joyous gathering and you will be surrounded by the people you love.

If your reading is primarily positive, then Berkana lets you know that success is highly probable. However, if you have got

an overall negative reading, that success might be temporary or short-lived.

Because Berkana portends new beginnings and is strongly associated with the feminine, women are especially susceptible to its influence. If you are a woman, you are in a wonderful position right now. Has there been a whisper from your 'inner voice' that you have been blocking? Now would be a perfect time to listen. Women's intuition is strengthened by the presence of Berkana.

If you have drawn the rune Ingwaz as well as Berkana, and you want to have children but have had problems conceiving, things could be about to change. Any troubles you may have experienced in the past are probably behind you.

PROSPERITY

Creation of a new life is not the only way that fertilization is manifested. You may have been kicking around an idea, a business plan or an interesting project recently. Having an upright

Berkana in your reading is a sign that you should trust this creative thought and make it reality. Although there may be obstacles along the way, the outcome has strong possibilities of success. If you believe in yourself and your idea, then nurture it into a thriving reality.

RELATIONSHIPS

New relationships must sometimes be treated like a newborn child. They must be tended and catered to, and energy must be spent in order to see them grow. If there is someone you want to be closer to, take this time to make an overture to them. Berkana is a rune of closeness, so it is an auspicious time to nurture a new relationship.

You are in a phase of fertility and rebirth. Use this creative spirit to advance yourself along the road to success. Remember to be true in your pursuit because deception usually foreshadows failure. Now is the time to open your heart to success, and it will enter.

BERKANA

REVERSED

A reversed Berkana shows that you might be at odds with your family. This is not a dire warning so much as a caution. Remember, these people are your support system. You are not compelled to agree with what they say, but don't alienate them. Talk to them and work towards understanding. If you can accomplish this, the rift will be short-lived.

Berkana reversed can also be a warning that trouble is on the way. There is the potential of something going wrong in the near future. There are even indications that someone in your family might experience an illness, or succumb to a 'disease of the spirit'. For the latter condition, kindness, understanding and unwavering support are yours to give.

If you have also drawn Gebo, the person you will most likely be concerned about will be your spouse or partner. With Ansuz it will be a child, and with Othala an older relative, such as one of your parents.

Pertaining to business, a reversed Berkana counsels caution. Your business will be safe as long as you practise good judgement, preparedness and timing. Don't discard your idea; rather, make sure you are ready for it. Just as you would not go to the opera wearing shorts (you would take the time to find out the correct attire), so you need to pay attention to your career. Do your homework and if things get put off for a short while, it is all right. Things could just work out better this way.

EHWAZ

UPRIGHT

SYMBOL OF TRAVEL, MOVEMENT AND LOYALTY

ORIGIN OF THE WORD: HORSE

The horse was the most common form of transport in ancient times and so Ehwaz is associated with travel and movement. A farmer uses his horse to plough his field. The counsel of Ehwaz is to work hard, be consistent and you too will make progress. Be the person on whom others can rely. Strive toward goals, not schemes or speculative ventures.

RELATIONSHIPS

The loyalty of a horse to its owner is another aspect of this rune. But Ehwaz is more than blind loyalty. Since horses were often with one owner for life, the togetherness of marriage is indicated. If you are currently married, then an upright Ehwaz shows a strengthening of the bonds that hold you together. If problems arise, your loyalty may be tested, but you will be able to prove to your spouse the depths of your feelings. If you are unmarried and seriously seeing someone, the subject of matrimony may start to enter your conversations. If there is loyalty between you, now is a good time to consider making your partnership a permanent one. If you are single and unattached, there could be a new lover in the near future.

PROSPERITY

This movement from one phase of a relationship to another extends to other areas of your life as well. There may be a promotion or a new job. You may move from a flat or apartment to a house, or from one home to another. These changes will not be made under stressful circumstances, but rather as a step toward your eventual goals. Ehwaz is a positive rune, so any movement will be good. You might get a better job, have a closer relationship or buy a house in a nicer neighbourhood. In some instances, it encompasses both physical and situational movement. Your new job could be in a different city,

or you might decide to move in with your lover. Again, these choices will usually be the right ones.

Another side of Ehwaz pertains to problem-solving. Whatever plan you make to cure a bad situation will be a good one. Your actions as well as your state of mind will bring success closer.

With Jera, Mannaz or Ansuz in your reading, you will get help from someone whose opinion carries weight with you. They will be someone you know and respect, possibly an older person. Their advice is wise and should be heeded.

TRAVEL

If Berkana or Raidho is in your reading, a pleasure trip may be coming. With an upright Ansuz, travel by land will be preferred. However, if Ansuz is reversed, you will probably need to travel to care for a relative or close friend.

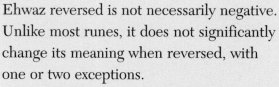

EHWAZ

REVERSED

Ehwaz reversed is not necessarily negative. Unlike most runes, it does not significantly change its meaning when reversed, with one or two exceptions.

A reversed Ehwaz indicates that you may be presented with an opportunity that is not necessarily the best thing for you at this time. Examine it closely. Is it a step forward, or does it really mean that you are standing still, or even taking a step backwards? If so, you should trust that something better will come along soon.

If you have a generally negative reading, Ehwaz is a warning to hold fast. This may not be the time for you to make any major changes in your life. They may complicate things and potentially damage the status quo. Be honest, because if you are true to yourself you are seldom wrong. Ehwaz does not talk about a timetable when things will get better. It is best to wait, and see what happens. Your natural insight will lead you to the problem that, once solved, will change everything.

When paired with some runes, a reversed Ehwaz can indicate a distant journey. With Laguz, you will most likely travel by air. If you drew Raidho, the journey is for recreation. With Fehu, it's an essential business trip. With Uruz, a change may come that will take you completely by surprise. However, Uruz's portent for change may be a detrimental one if you have a negative reading.

MANNAZ

UPRIGHT

SYMBOL OF HUMANKIND AND INTERDEPENDENCE

ORIGIN OF THE WORD: HUMANKIND

With very few exceptions, humankind lives and works as a societal group. You are an individual, but you don't stand alone. In ancient times, survival depended on tribal unity. It took coordinated skills to have the necessities of life. It is this interdependency that is the basis of the rune Mannaz.

ADVICE

The promise of Mannaz arrives in the form of advice and assistance. It is time to seek the counsel of someone who is in a position to help you. Listen carefully to their advice, for it will be trustworthy and unbiased, with no ulterior motive.

DELAYS

If you drew delay runes, it is probably not a good time for you to start new projects. Important decisions should also be put on hold. You will know when the timing is right if you believe in yourself. If you have questions, ask that trustworthy adviser.

SELF-INVOLVED

You may have become too involved with your present problems and are now so consumed by them that you have lost sight of how to solve them. The realities of the situation may not be as bad as you believe them to be. You have become so self-involved that you have lost touch with your true inner self. Self-involved does not mean self-discerning. One clear way to improve your position is to adopt a positive attitude. Take a moment to visualize solutions. Use your mind's eye to see yourself out of your current predicament. Now is also a good time to seek the advice alluded to earlier. If you have drawn Ansuz, the advice will come from a conversation with someone older and wiser. Remember that no one is an island, so look to others for help.

RELATIONSHIPS

You are now at a point in your life where tolerance of others is key. If you have found yourself to be judgemental, now is the time to eliminate this from your psyche. As you judge others, so others will judge you. Learn acceptance of all of humankind's variety and you will find yourself accepted and beloved in kind.

Mannaz is a positive rune because it gives several ways to improve your current situation. You can ask others for help and advice and visualize the solutions to problems. Another necessary ingredient is humility. Don't openly brag of your accomplishments, because those you want to impress will not take it in a good light. View your situation with a clear, logical eye. Put passion aside for a moment and distance yourself so that you can see the larger picture. You are surrounded by friendly members of humankind who want you to be your best. Remember, you are not alone in this complex world of ours.

MANNAZ
REVERSED

Mannaz reversed indicates that you are standing alone, without help from anyone. Whether it is a group or a single person, you may have an enemy or a detractor. Don't be paranoid, but be aware of what is going on around you. Blind trust without any awareness is not serving you at this time.

Sometimes a reversed Mannaz can mean you are your own worst enemy. Self-doubt or a gloomy outlook on life can make things seem worse than they really are. Conceit or stubbornness may be to blame, or it could just be a generally negative attitude. Try to see things from another person's perspective. Do your best to acknowledge all the positive things in your life. With practice, you can begin to shake off that pervasive gloom.

Your life may have a strange, foreign feel to it. You may have recently moved house or returned from a place where customs are different. Perhaps there is someone whose thoughts and actions seem strange or foreign to you. Whatever the case, the differences between you will cause anxiety. You may be timid, fearing you will offend this person with your behaviour or make a cultural error. Yet there is the fascination of being with someone so different. You might find yourself inexplicably attracted to him or her. This could end in mild flirtation, sexual interest or a romance. The outcome of this relationship will depend on your ability to readjust and synthesize yourself back into society.

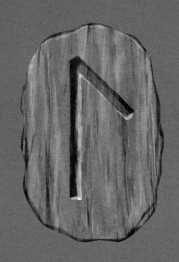

LAGUZ

UPRIGHT

SYMBOL OF INTUITION AND YOUR INNER VOICE

ORIGIN OF THE WORD: WATER

Have you ever dreamed something that came true? Ever felt certain about a decision, despite advice to the contrary? These experiences fall under what is known as innate or intuitive knowledge. The rune Laguz stands for these feelings. It is a gut feeling that can tell you when something is right or wrong.

There are times when you *know* someone is lying to you, or perhaps you recall feeling that a situation was not what it seemed to be. It is like an inexplicable psychic awareness, an eerie knowledge that something is about to happen. It is your 'inner voice'. Laguz counsels you to pay close attention to it, because guidance can come from unusual sources. Even if you have doubted your intuition in the past, now is the time to put your trust in it.

CREATIVITY

When you speak to people who are successful members of the creative community and ask them where they get their ideas, they will often be unable to explain. Creativity and the inner voice are closely tied. You are now entering a very creative phase. Your inner voice is going to be more active and the ideas will flow readily. Painting, writing, dancing, music – all can be heightened, depending on your abilities. If you are an actor, you will enter an especially good time. The meaning of the word Laguz is 'water', and ideas can surge in waves like water. Another aspect of liquid is its ability to take the form of any vessel in which it is placed. As an actor, you must strive to flow into the form of the character you play.

INTUITION

If you are female, listen to your female intuition. You can count on this guidance to help you make the right decisions. Laguz is the primary feminine rune and your strength is at its peak. If you are male and drew Laguz, there is probably a woman in your life who has strong feelings and is tuned in on a level at which you are not.

There is always a need for imaginative approaches to problem-solving. The most obvious course of action may not be the best. At this time, it would be wise to think in an abstract manner. Again, listen to that voice from within and you will know what is right.

TRANSITIONS

Any downward cycles are near an end. It is time for you to re-evaluate your situation. A spring-cleaning of your life is in order. After all, you need to be prepared for the upward turn your life will soon be taking. If you are at college or at a new position or job, use your excellent memory. Success will come that much quicker if you do. Make influential contacts and get yourself noticed. With confidence tempered by humility, you will be unstoppable.

LAGUZ

REVERSED

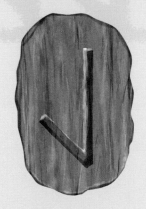

When Laguz is reversed, you have an inner voice that is giving you bad advice. Through either ego or conceit, you are now in way over your head. It is time to be honest with yourself and re-evaluate the situation.

You might be trying to shift responsibility to another's shoulders. Unless you face things head on and take all the necessary steps, you will be caught. You could lose more than money, love or prestige: you are in danger of losing your self-respect. Step back from the problem, ignore your inner voice and look at this as if you were an outsider. What would a stranger think?

If you are a man, a woman in your life will bring trouble. She may be able to help with a problem, but you will pay dearly for it. If you are a woman, it is important to focus on tangible things and not on any intuitive feelings you may have about what is happening.

This can change. Be truthful with yourself, know your limitations yet strive to extend them. Pay attention to what is really going on around you, look closely at the motivations of others, and avoid the easy solution. You have what it takes.

If you have an extremely positive runecast, most of the sting is taken out of Laguz reversed. Major areas of your life will not be affected. Only minor, possibly frustrating, inconveniences will result, and not dire consequences. Be patient with yourself and others and you will succeed.

INGWAZ

**SYMBOL OF COMPLETION AND
NEW BEGINNINGS**

**ORIGIN OF THE WORD: THE GOD
ING**

Ing was a hero of the ancient
Danes. Having no reverse,
Ingwaz is a good stone to draw
and is most commonly seen as
a transitional rune. It is a
symbol of completion. Having
accomplished your goals, you
can now bask in your success.
It puts an end to the stress that
goes with accomplishing
difficult tasks.

TRANSITIONS

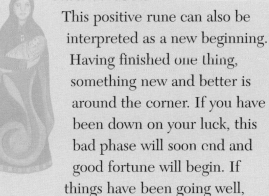

This positive rune can also be
interpreted as a new beginning.
Having finished one thing,
something new and better is
around the corner. If you have
been down on your luck, this
bad phase will soon end and
good fortune will begin. If
things have been going well,
they are about to get even better.

You may also be about to reach a
milestone in your life. If you have a fertility
rune, it may indicate the birth of a child.
Prosperity runes could indicate a new job
or a different position at your current place
of employment. Relationship runes may
mean a new romance brewing in the near
future. If you are already happily married,
then your current relationship will enter
exciting unexplored territory.

DELAY

The cyclical power of Ingwaz can help
things come to fruition. For example, there
are times when you might have a good
idea, but it is only a vague outline. Instead
of trying to implement something that is

incomplete, you should put it on the 'back burner' of your mind. Later, the idea will return with form and substance.

If you have a negative reading, Ingwaz is probably referring to something that didn't work out. As with any disappointment, you can learn from the experience. Think of your last project or romance: what went wrong? You can end the negative cycle and leave yourself better prepared for future challenges.

MORE TRANSITIONS

This is a rune of change, completion and new beginnings, and therefore you may be required to divest yourself of some old baggage. It may be a job that no longer suits you, a relationship that has run its course or even your own definition of yourself. The past is the past, and it is time for you to make a fresh start. Like a reptile shedding its skin in order to grow, you can thank that once-needed thing or person for being there for you in your old life. But now you need to prepare for a rebirth. You are about to start a brand-new cycle, with new experiences and new people. Embrace this change, for it is far more suited to the person you are today than that old layer of skin you are now ready to shed.

DAGAZ

SYMBOL OF PROSPERITY, GROWTH AND SECURITY

ORIGIN OF THE WORD: DAY

To the ancients, daytime was for work and social interaction. With no electricity to elongate the day, darkness was for sleep and rejuvenation. Dagaz is the symbol for light, prosperity, fruitfulness, security, increase and growth. It has no reverse and its powerful energy can transcend other negative stones. Dagaz implies a positive outcome to any problem.

PROSPERITY

Dagaz predicts a period of prosperity. This is not winning the lottery, but rather the kind of abundance that comes after hard work. It is a slow but steady increase that, in the long run, markedly changes your life. In fact, you may not even notice the steady growth, but one day you will see that the difference is like night and day.

RELATIONSHIPS

These positive changes also take place on a personal level. It could mean that your feelings for the person you have been seeing for a while will blossom into heartfelt love. Your entire attitude towards life, business, friendship and romance can change to a lighter, more positive, outlook. This 'lightness' will then draw people and opportunities to you. What seems good now will only get better.

TRANSITIONS

Dagaz can also mean a new start. The life that you now know may be gone for ever.

What replaces it will be better than it ever was. This change in attitude will open new doors and experiences. Overall, this is a time for you to accept these possibilities and let them grow into a positive new life.

If your reading is negative, you may be unaware that changes are taking place all around you. Such changes are often subtle, but ultimately they will make things better. You have the inner strength to prevail. Eventually, given some time, you will prove to be victorious over a situation that now seems irreversible.

If you have drawn Hagalaz or a reversed Wunjo, Mannaz or Othala, it is best not to think about your problems too much. It will only make things worse. Remember, if you dwell on a problem, you will only draw it closer to you. It is always wise to let go of a problem once you have done all that you possibly can to solve it. It may be time to move on.

PROTECTION

Apprehension and fear often precede change and growth, but now there is no need for these feelings. Dagaz also means security. As daylight keeps the predators away, so will your spirit be protected. The changes predicted here will not be filled with unnecessary risk. Rather, they will be earned by your energetic work and honest heart. You can be secure in the fact that you deserve what is coming.

OTHALA

UPRIGHT

SYMBOL OF MATERIAL POSSESSIONS, CHARACTER AND INHERITANCE

ORIGIN OF THE WORD: POSSESSION

Othala is the rune that symbolizes possessions or things that money can buy. Since land was a form of wealth in early civilizations, Othala commonly refers to land and the structures on that land. The family home is still considered as wealth today, usually in the form of equity for a loan or as an inheritance.

PROSPERITY

Othala may refer to money. Not money in the form of liquid assets, but as trust funds, pensions, stocks or other investments. These are items of wealth that are in your possession but not necessarily accessible.

It is wise to be rather cautious in your relationship with money. If you are too materialistic, some people might think you are cheap or tight-fisted. Loosen up. There

is more to life than possessions, money and uncontrolled greed. In combination with victory runes, Othala shows you are a hard worker. You are not afraid to give your all and enjoy the benefits this gives you. Just be careful not to become addicted to work.

IDEALISM

You may be the type of person who lives to fight for social causes. You may, in fact, be so possessed by your own ideals that you care for little else. Although this 'tunnel vision' can reap great benefits – focused concentration can often accomplish the seemingly impossible – it can lead to a life without variety. Remember, it is not a crime to take a day off, enjoy a hobby, go on holiday or have outside interests.

INHERITANCE

Another aspect of Othala is inheritance, but this brings with it the spectre of loss. In order to inherit money or property, someone must die. Therefore, the property alluded to may carry a loss with it. For

example, if you were to move to a place where you own property, you could lose the friends you left behind, some of the value on your old house, proximity to your family or even a cherished career.

Othala is not necessarily limited to tangible items. Your legacy could be that of inherited characteristics, personality traits or behavioural patterns. Because Othala is upright, these characteristics will prove to be of great benefit to you. You might even carry these traits with you for the rest of your life.

Knowledge can be seen as great wealth, since it has accrued over time. Therefore, you may be the recipient of learned guidance from an older, wiser and trusted relation. This assistance could also come from old friends, a long-established company or civic organization, a church or synagogue, or even the government. Treasure this knowledge, for it is now part of your inheritance.

OTHALA
REVERSED

Othala reversed is usually a sign of frustration and delay. You may be trying to move too fast. If you persist on going at high speeds, you may destroy any chance of reaching your goals. If you have an otherwise positive reading, you will probably achieve them. It will simply take you a little longer than you estimated.

The timetable you have set may be out of step with reality. Don't be so hurried that you can't see opportunities. Rushing from project to project, or relationship to relationship, can blind you. Given the proper amount of time, things will fall into place. If something is immediate, remember to pay close attention to details. Brushing aside the essential, but time-consuming, details is

the surest way to sabotage anything that has great potential.

You might be standing alone. Your haste, actions and goals may have alienated you from your friends, family or business associates. Unfortunately, help will not be forthcoming from the usual places in which you have sought it in the past. Money won't help you out of the fix you may be in, either. Sincerity will get you a lot farther than a cheque. Honesty will win the day.

Now is the time to slow down and implement a more conservative approach. This may be all you need to fix things. If not, it is an excellent place from which to start. Let your inner truths show, and it is difficult for anyone to resist.

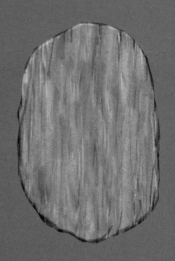

WYRD

SYMBOL OF KARMIC FATE
ORIGIN OF THE WORD: THE NORNS

Wyrd (pronounced 'weird') is a rune that has its basis in Norse mythology, but is a recent addition to the futhark. Wyrd is based on the three mythological sisters known as the Norns. They were Urdhr (past), Verthandi (present) and Skuld (future). Together they represent ever-evolving time and all things known and unknown. If you wish, remove Wyrd from your set.

KARMA

Wyrd is as the rune of karmic fate. Karma means that the quality of your present and future lives are influenced by your behaviour in this and past lives. Since karma assumes reincarnation, it speaks of an accrued 'account' from one life to another. Karma is a concept in which you are in control of your own destiny and responsible for the things that take place in your life.

The theory of karma is one of cause and effect. What you have already done in the past is unchangeable. If there are unpleasant actions, then these will be repaid at some time in your life (or lives). However, you *can* control the present and the future. Wyrd's appearance is a reminder that good works today, tomorrow and forever will also be repaid. Think of life as an opportunity to be the best kind of person you can be.

UNKNOWN

Wyrd is a void. It is both nothing and everything. It refers to the unknown factors in your life that might be meant to remain unknown. It also points to times when

milestones are reached and things are never the same again. It draws meaning from other stones or its position in your runecast. It leaves most of its meaning to your interpretation of things such as fate and karma. It is up to you to decide on the importance of these concepts and what role they play in your life.

Look at the other runes you have drawn, and, based on their meanings, you must extrapolate what Wyrd is trying to tell you. For example, if you drew Gebo, you may be rewarded by a new love interest. But if you drew a reversed Algiz, you may be due some karmic payback for taking advantage of your friends. With a delay rune, it may be telling you that your karma is not yet ready to manifest. If Wyrd landed in the future or result position, there may be no easy answer for your current situation.

It is up to you, using your insight and instincts, to interpret Wyrd's influence and its meaning. Take a deep breath, look into the void of this rune's empty face and perhaps your heart, mind and soul will understand some of its mysteries.

USING RUNES FOR POSITIVE CHANGE

Now that you are familiar with the runes, it is time to use them as a means

of divination and self-exploration. Interpreting the runes takes an open

mind, a little common sense and a touch of magic. You have the tools and

the desire, so prepare to unlock some secrets.

USING RUNES TO UNDERSTAND YOURSELF

To tap into the divine mysteries embodied by the runes, it is important that you have a sense of understanding about yourself. To achieve this, you can use the runes themselves as your guide.

Because there is no way to know exactly how the ancient runemasters laid out their stones, modern runecasters have borrowed from other divinatory sources, such as the Tarot and the I-Ching. These other spreads work well with the runes, but this modern 'borrowing' means that layouts are open to interpretation, new forms and your own insightful imagination. Feel free to create your own layouts that specifically respond to your concerns, questions and lifestyle.

When you begin reading the runes, you can choose a layout that is as simple or as complex as you prefer. You can ask a yes or no question and draw a rune. If it is upright, the answer is yes. If it is reversed, it is no. If it is a rune without a reverse, you can either assume you must ask the question later or draw another stone.

To get the full value out of the runes' potential, you will need to learn how to do layouts and interpretations.

To begin your voyage of self-discovery, ask the runes if the time is right. When you have concentrated on this question, shake your rune pouch to mix up the stones and then reach into the bag, sifting through them until one piece 'feels' like the answer. Pull it out and see if it is upright or reversed. If your runes have no clear north–south orientation, and your rune is sideways, move it one-quarter clockwise. If it is upright, it is time to begin. Replace the stone.

ONE-STONE READING: 'WHO AM I?'

Focus on a new question. Ask the runes who you are at this moment in your life. This will be your 'base'. It may tell you the positive things you bring to the world, or it could highlight some of the challenges in your life. You will be the best person to interpret how its meaning applies to your question. Pull a new stone from the bag.

SAMPLE READING
UPRIGHT EHWAZ

Ehwaz is the rune that stands for 'horse' and signifies travel, movement and loyalty. Let's pretend for a moment that as you begin on your spiritual path of self-discovery, you drew this stone. If you read about an upright Ehwaz, you will see that it covers more than one category, such as prosperity and relationships. These all contribute to that picture of the self that you can derive from a one-stone reading.

You might feel that some of the details hit home, while others don't appear to apply as neatly. This is normal. Not every truth is self-evident, so the hidden aspects may become clearer with time. Sometimes you pull a stone for one statement or aspect that resonates deeply within you. If you need to hear something, the runes will tell you, even if you were not expecting that answer. Keep an open mind.

Nearly any question can be answered with a single stone. The answer may not be complex, but the rune will give you insights.

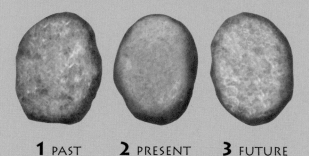

1 PAST   **2** PRESENT   **3** FUTURE

THREE-STONE READING: 'WHERE AM I?'

It is important to get a sense of where you are in time and this means gaining insight into how you to got to where you are today, your present circumstances and a glimpse into a possible future. For this, you can use

SAMPLE READING
REVERSED RAIDHO, UPRIGHT KENAZ, JERA

Here the past shows a reversed Raidho, the present shows an upright Kenaz and the future shows Jera, a stone with no reverse.

The reversed Raidho speaks of difficulties in the past, possibly involving travel or perhaps indicating a plan that went awry. If these were the stones you drew, you should study the description of Raidho in this book, both upright and reversed, to familiarize yourself with the symbol and its meanings. Then you should contemplate how the message of the reversed Raidho applies to

you. When you feel the resonance of the rune, and its message, it is time to move on to the stone sitting in the 'present' position.

An upright Kenaz is a wonderfully positive rune. Again, if this reading were about you, you would study the meaning and apply it to your life. Drawing Kenaz, a rune of health, creativity and relationships, would probably mean these things are a focus in the present. Think about what is going on in your life, and try to discern those places in which the rune description and your life events intersect.

the layout of the Norns, showing the past, present and future.

For learning's sake, I'll draw three runes and we'll pretend that they apply to you. In this way you will see what different thought processes you need to go through as you use the runes.

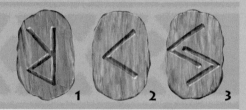

Think about the effect a reversed Raidho in the past might have on an upright Kenaz in the present. Can you see a correlation? Can you see the flow of one rune to another, and how they can influence each other? These are the kinds of questions you should ask yourself when you do your own reading.

Finally, it is time to examine the rune that landed in the future, or result, position. This is Jera, a rune with no reverse. Jera is a cycle rune, and a symbol of the harvest. It shows a reaping of rewards from hard work.

Putting all three stones together, there is a pattern of missed opportunities leading to a focus on personal creativity, which results in the reaping of rewards. This is a kind of roadmap that your life may have followed, had these been the runes you drew.

Like the one-stone read, you can ask any question and use the three-stone layout. It gives a quick, yet more detailed answer than a single rune, and is an excellent way to get an overview of where you or another questioner stands in time.

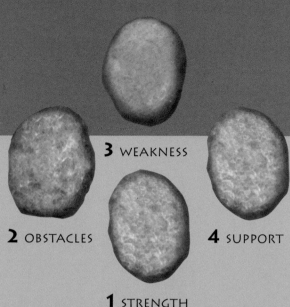

3 WEAKNESS

2 OBSTACLES

4 SUPPORT

1 STRENGTH

FOUR-STONE READING: 'WHAT ARE MY PERSONAL STRENGTHS AND CHALLENGES?'

Now that you know who and where you are, it is time to take a more detailed approach to flesh out the simple answers.

SAMPLE READING
UPRIGHT LAGUZ, REVERSED MANNAZ, DAGAZ, UPRIGHT FEHU

Jenny is at a crossroads in her life and wants to know what strengths and challenges she has. Using the four-stone reading, she received an upright Laguz in the strength position, a reversed Mannaz in obstacles, Dagaz in weakness and an upright Fehu in the support position.

Starting with Laguz in the strength position, it is easy to see that Jenny's strengths are creativity, imagination and intuition – a wonderful set of skills to bring to the world – and it is also easy to see why these would be considered strengths.

Travelling clockwise from Laguz, we find a reversed Mannaz in the obstacles position. This rune speaks of self-doubt, conceit, a gloomy outlook or the presence of an enemy. These are the things standing in Jenny's way.

From obstacles, we go to weaknesses and see Dagaz. Because Dagaz is such a strong, positive rune, Jenny didn't understand how it could show weakness. The idea is to read the information on Dagaz knowing that it is talking about a weakness. The positives it espouses are most likely things that are within her grasp, if she can overcome her

A four-stone reading would work well here. Designed to help you discover your current condition, this layout points out your strengths and weaknesses, as well as obstacles and possible sources of support. When you pull the runes, start at the bottom and place each subsequent rune clockwise around the layout until you have all four.

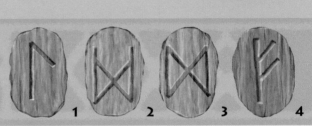

1 2 3 4

vulnerabilities. For example, it speaks of earning rewards from hard work. Is Jenny working hard enough or is she dreaming of rewards while being unwilling to do the work? Perhaps she is dwelling on her problems and attracting more to her. This is another weakness that must be overcome.

Now that she has seen strengths and weaknesses, along with obstacles, it's time to explore what kind of support she can expect. The final rune is an upright Fehu, which shows that there is support out there. Interestingly, this rune also speaks of rewards after hard work. Because this concept came up twice, Jenny needs to look at this as a possible issue. Fehu also gives information on relationships – another good source of support.

When Jenny finished exploring each individual rune's meaning, she then looked at the reading as a whole and gained valuable insight into her strengths and challenges. She is now aware of what she needs to do to achieve her goals. Like Jenny, you too can gain a powerful perspective with this layout.

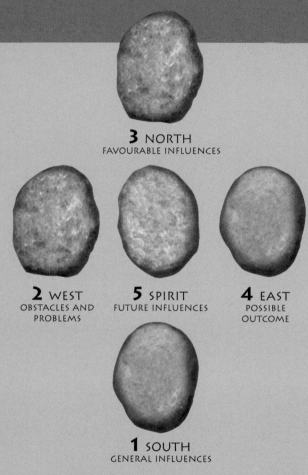

3 NORTH
FAVOURABLE INFLUENCES

2 WEST
OBSTACLES AND
PROBLEMS

5 SPIRIT
FUTURE INFLUENCES

4 EAST
POSSIBLE
OUTCOME

1 SOUTH
GENERAL INFLUENCES

move to the centre. Each of the positions has an additional meaning: south is also general influences; west is obstacles and problems; north is favourable influences; east is possible outcome; and spirit is also future influences.

The more stones you lay out, the more complex the messages from the runes will be. Yet it is not difficult to find the overall trends and patterns. You can ask any question of the Thor's Cross and the answer will be written in the runes. Don't fear the complexity, rather welcome it, since the more you know, the more you will understand about the influences that affect you and your world.

FIVE-STONE READING:
'WHAT INFLUENCES AFFECT MY LIFE?'

A good layout to track the influences on your life is Thor's Cross. This is a five-stone reading and incorporates the four points on a compass. As you can see, the directional stones surround a central 'spirit' stone to give you the reading. Again, start with the bottom, southern stone, and move clockwise to west, north and east, and then

EIHWAZ, REVERSED NAUTHIZ, REVERSED OTHALA, UPRIGHT ALGIZ, GEBO

William is having some difficulties and wants to know which influences are affecting his life. Using Thor's Cross, I drew five stones, keeping William's problems in mind. Starting with the southern stone, Eihwaz shows what the general influences are. This is a good, strong rune that has no reverse. It does, however, mention several times that there will be obstacles. The next stone in the western spot is in the obstacle position, which means the two runes will exert a strong influence on each other. Eihwaz shows the presence of protection, flexibility and endurance in the general influences, all of which will be needed to overcome obstacles.

A reversed Nauthiz, a powerful delay rune, is in the obstacle position. It also speaks of obstacles in many areas, including health and relationships. This could make it overwhelming due to its placement, but because Eihwaz is there to help with the delays, they balance each other out.

Going from west to north, we find a reversed Othala in the spot related to favourable influences. William wondered why something 'favourable' held a reversed rune. Othala is a prosperity rune that, when reversed, warns of delays. It also cautions against trying to go so fast that William can miss opportunities. Why is this favourable? Because if he heeds its warnings, he will be in a position to take advantage of opportunities he might otherwise miss.

So far, all three stones have warned of delays. By now, that message for William should be crystal clear. So what will

CONTINUED NEXT PAGE

SAMPLE READING CONTINUED:

1   2   3   4   5

happen if these warnings are heeded, using the strengths outlined in the general influences? The answer is in the eastern stone, which shows the possible outcome – only 'possible', because it depends on whether he listens to the advice of the other runes.

An upright Algiz is a wonderful stone to get in the result position. It speaks of something new and exciting coming into William's life. It may be a new friend, or a new opportunity, but whatever it is, it will be a positive influence on his future. This might be the opportunity that he would have missed, as portended by the reversed Othala.

And finally, it's time to look at the centre stone. This is the spirit stone, which indicates future influences. Another positive rune, Gebo is a true gift in this reading. It is a relationship rune, which should immediately bring to mind one of the messages of the upright Algiz, the 'friendship' rune. If that new, important person does make an appearance, he or she will be a very positive influence on William's future.

FIVE-STONE READING:
'HOW CAN I DEEPEN MY SPIRITUAL
UNDERSTANDING?'

There is a lot of flexibility in the layouts used for runes. What if you want to do a five-stone reading, but Thor's Cross, although close, does not quite seem as if it will hold the answers you seek? You have some choices. You can do a different five-stone layout, decide to draw more or fewer stones, or you can adapt the pattern you were originally drawn to, Thor's Cross, and change the meanings of the various positions and the order of the draw.

For example, instead of using the directional compass, you can use the elements. Here is the same layout you just saw, and yet the meanings of the positions of the various stones are different. Another sample reading, using this new interpretation, will show how differently two readings, both using five stones in the same pattern, can be. The question this time is 'How can I deepen my spiritual understanding?' Lay out the stones, starting at the top this time, and work clockwise, drawing the centre stone last.

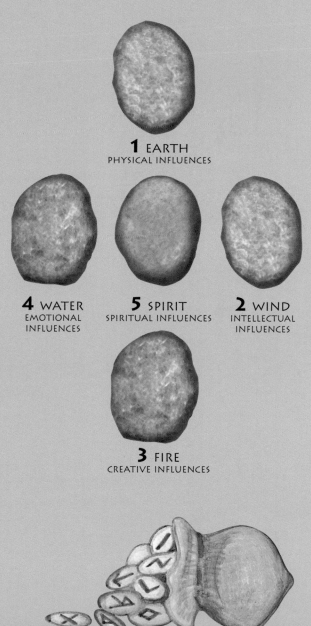

1 EARTH
PHYSICAL INFLUENCES

4 WATER
EMOTIONAL
INFLUENCES

5 SPIRIT
SPIRITUAL INFLUENCES

2 WIND
INTELLECTUAL
INFLUENCES

3 FIRE
CREATIVE INFLUENCES

UPRIGHT BERKANA, UPRIGHT URUZ, REVERSED PERTHRO, UPRIGHT RAIDHO, REVERSED TIWAZ

Donna is the subject of this reading, as she searches for answers to a spiritual crisis. She has drawn Berkana in the earth (physical) position, Uruz in wind (intellectual), a reversed Perthro in fire (creative), Raidho in water (emotional) and, finally, a reversed Tiwaz in spirit.

The first stone, Berkana, alludes to Donna's body and physical surroundings. It is a stone of rebirth, fertility and family. Berkana is a feminine rune, so Donna should be especially heedful of its message. Because it includes her environment, the 'new beginning' might mean a change of address, a new addition to her house or some other impact on the physical world around her. Because her question was about deepening her

spiritual understanding, the implication is that the new beginning in the physical plane will have an influence on the spiritual plane. Sometimes, a person can change one small thing and it will have a domino effect on many other aspects of their life. Perhaps the other runes in the reading will help Donna key in on some of these threads.

Moving to the second stone, an upright Uruz stands in the wind, or intellectual influences, spot. This masculine rune represents strength and change. The new beginning that was portended by Berkana is now being reinforced by Uruz. This stone shows that the intellectual strength Donna needs to meet the new challenge will be there. Uruz signals robust health (in this case it would be the health of Donna's mind) and also adaptability. This rune is a good omen for her.

1 2 3 4 5

However, when we look at the fire rune, we see a reversed Perthro. This rune of secrets and hidden things has landed in the spot for creative influences. Perhaps these hidden truths are standing in the way of Donna's spiritual understanding. She needs to face those secrets, and own up to whatever negativity is attached to them, so that she can clear a path for her new beginning.

The emotional influences, represented by an upright Raidho in the water spot, again focuses on movement. This travelling rune speaks of spiritual quests, logical thought and physical journeys. This bodes well for Donna's emotional stability.

With a place in the layout that predicts spiritual influences, and Donna's quest to find deeper understanding of the spiritual, it is not good news to see one of the strongest runes, Tiwaz, reversed. This is a fairly clear

indication that her spiritual quest probably won't begin until those secrets Perthro suggested are cleared up. Her spirit knows when she is facing the world honestly and when she is holding harmful energy inside her. The lethargy and miscommunication predicted by Tiwaz cannot be expelled until the first stop on her spiritual journey is reached – a look at her own inner truths and accepting responsibility for them. When that happens, the new beginning can start.

Unlike the last five-stone reading, which had many delays, this five-stone reading showed a trend towards change, movement and new beginnings. It's important to remember that the stones you pick will depend on your question and on the energy you bring to the runes. It isn't the layout that will determine the trends, the message or the influences, it is the stones.

USING THESE LAYOUTS

A journey of self-understanding is an excellent way to begin your relationship with the runes. The more you understand, the better the runes will serve you. One way to keep in touch with this self-understanding is to start every day with a quick one-rune reading, asking 'Who am I today?'. This will give you a barometer for the day, helping you to understand some of the actions and reactions you will experience as the day progresses.

At the end of the day, a three-stone 'Where am I?' reading could help you process the day's activities. How did your experiences that day affect you? Were there any hidden lessons that you needed to learn? The runes may be able to shine a light on thoughts and events that you had not fully integrated. If you are faced with a difficult decision, a check of your strengths and challenges might give you the insight you need to make up your mind. If you pull delay runes, it can tell you that the decision is better left to another time, when you are stronger and more capable of making a decision that is beneficial to everyone involved.

ONE-STONE READING

THREE-STONE READING

The five-stone reading, Thor's Cross, is always helpful, regardless of what you are facing. It is important to know the things that are influencing you and might be leading you towards actions that might be beneficial, or could be detrimental. To assess all of the influences that come into play – physical, intellectual, creative, emotional and spiritual – the alternative layout of the five-stone reading is helpful. Sometimes it is important to get a well-rounded view of which forces are at work.

Once you have finished the exploration of your inner self, it will be time to move on to new explorations. In the next section, you will see how to guide your present life using a new set of layouts, both large and small. You will see many of the same runes that were shown in this section, but their interpretations will depend on the questions asked and also on their positions in the layouts. I hope this will help you when you begin to ask your own questions and draw your own runes.

FIVE-STONE READING: THOR'S CROSS

USING RUNES TO GUIDE YOUR PRESENT LIFE

When many people seek the advice of an oracle, they are primarily concerned about something specific that is occurring in their life at that moment. These include questions about health, relationships, finances, careers, spirituality and general problems or concerns.

When you seek the counsel of the runes, these will probably comprise the bulk of your questions. Concern for the immediate is only natural. It is those day-to-day questions of living, working and loving that can fill your mind at any given moment. It is helpful to have something that can give you guidance, whether your current problems are petty or life-changing.

When people find out you are working with an oracle, curiosity often gets the better of them. They, too, want the guidance and the illumination the runes can provide. Don't be surprised if you get several requests for divination.

As before, you can decide how detailed you want the answers to be. Using fewer stones means a more general reading, while using more stones gives a more targeted answer. For the casual question of an acquaintance, a simple layout might suffice. It will give this person something to look at in his or her life, and won't tax your time or abilities. But you might desire a far more detailed look into your own problems, influences, obstacles and strengths.

In this section, I will introduce you to more layouts, and will use more sample questions to help you familiarize yourself with rune interpretation.

1 DAY/POSITIVE   **2** NIGHT/NEGATIVE

TWO-STONE READING:
'WHAT IS MY LESSON TODAY?'

You could answer a question like this with a one-stone reading, getting a simple overview of the day, but you might want a little more information than that. Life lessons are composed of both positive and negative energy. You exalt in the positives and should learn from the negatives. These two poles are represented by day and night, light and dark, positive and negative. This layout is different from most, because the orientation of the stone won't necessarily remain as you have drawn it.

Using the question 'What is my lesson today?', pull two stones, placing the first on the left and the second on the right. Pay close attention to their orientation.

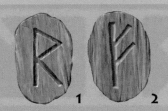

SAMPLE READING
UPRIGHT RAIDHO, UPRIGHT FEHU

Arthur has drawn an upright Raidho in the day position and an upright Fehu in the night position. Raidho then represents the positive influences and the upright Fehu represents the negative. 'What is negative about an upright Fehu?' asks Arthur. This is where this layout differs from others. The day position should hold a positive stone, and the night position should hold a negative stone. Arthur flips the rune in the night position, so that it becomes a reversed Fehu.

Now he has an upright rune in the positive position and a reversed rune in the negative position. However, there must have been a reason that Fehu was drawn

CONTINUED → NEXT PAGE

upright. This needs to be acknowledged. Therefore, in Arthur's reading, the day rune will have a stronger influence than the night when he interprets the stones.

The same logic applies had he pulled a reversed rune in the positive position (upend the reversed rune and give it less weight). If both are opposite, reverse them and treat them with equal weight. If both land correctly, treat them equally. If he had drawn a stone that had no reverse, such as Gebo, Sowilo or Isa, he could either put it back and draw again, or interpret it as his intuition told him.

In Arthur's current reading, the upright Raidho in the stronger, positive position is a rune of travel and movement. He needs to be aware of communication (telephone, email or letters) and any travelling he might do that day. Even a short trip could be significant if he is observant. Because Raidho predicts heightened skills of communication and negotiation, it would also be an excellent day for Arthur to clear up misunderstandings or talk business.

What are the negative influences? The reversed Fehu warns of financial loss and delays. But because the stronger influence of Raidho alleviates some of the warnings found in a reversed Fehu, Arthur should be able to avoid the more dangerous traps. For example, if he discusses business, he needs to pay close attention to the financial details. If there is a misunderstanding, he should look for the deeper issues and deal directly with them, instead of the surface complaints. With only two stones, Arthur has found some solid advice, has put some possible dangers in the spotlight and has the tools to deal with any surprises.

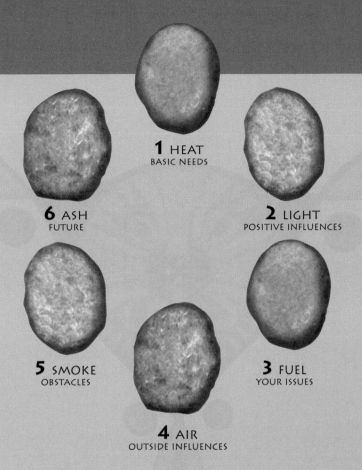

1 HEAT
BASIC NEEDS

6 ASH
FUTURE

2 LIGHT
POSITIVE INFLUENCES

5 SMOKE
OBSTACLES

3 FUEL
YOUR ISSUES

4 AIR
OUTSIDE INFLUENCES

SIX-STONE READING:
'WHAT IS THE BEST WAY TO DEAL
WITH THIS SITUATION?'

There will be many times when you are faced with a difficult situation that you don't know how to resolve. If you want to seek the guidance of the runes, then a good layout is the Campfire, or Hearth Stones, spread. Six runes are laid out in a circular pattern reminiscent of the stones around an open fire. The ancients spent many an evening sitting around their hearths, talking, eating, arguing – in short, doing the things that people do everywhere. If they had a problem, it is likely that, more than once, difficulties were discussed and possibly solved by the light of the campfire.

Each of the positions stands for an aspect of the hearth – heat, light, fuel, air, smoke and, when it is extinguished, ash. For this layout, begin at the top with heat and move clockwise around the circle.

UPRIGHT OTHALA, UPRIGHT TIWAZ, ISA, UPRIGHT THURISAZ, UPRIGHT FEHU, JERA

For our sample reading, we need to identify what the 'situation' in the question is. Say there is a dispute between Mary and her neighbour. The neighbour has several large trees that were damaged by a storm, but he refuses to cut away the dead branches. However, if the branches were to fall, they could damage Mary's house. The two neighbours have reached an impasse. Mary wants to know how to reconcile the dispute without further aggravating relations between them. Thinking about Mary's situation, I drew the runes shown here.

The first thing you will probably notice is how positive the reading appears. There are no reversed stones, and it includes some very strong, positive runes. Mary appears to be in

a very good position. But this is no simple yes or no question. You must look below the surface and seek out the trends. Hopefully, a clear picture of how to resolve the dispute between the neighbours will emerge.

Starting at the top with the heat position (basic needs) we find an upright Othala. You can tell immediately that the reading is on the right track, because one of Othala's meanings is material possessions, in particular, one's home and the land surrounding it. Houses and shelter are indeed 'basic needs'. The upright Othala assures Mary that her home and property stand strong and she has what it takes to provide her own basic needs. Because her home is what is threatened, the upright Othala is a good omen. Perhaps this

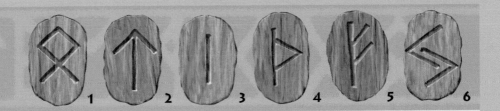

1   2   3   4   5   6

dispute with her neighbour can be settled to everyone's satisfaction.

Othala includes a meaning of acquired wisdom by seeking guidance from someone older and wiser. Perhaps Mary's first step should be to seek the advice of someone she trusts. The other stones should give us some insight as to whom this person should be.

Moving on to the next position, light (positive influences), we find an extremely strong rune – an upright Tiwaz. This victory rune assures Mary that she will prevail in her fight. Most likely,

there will be a man helping her in the battle, since Tiwaz is a male rune. Adding this to the suggestion to seek advice, it appears that whoever that person is, he should be male. Mary can add this clue and take heart in the strength that Tiwaz lends the runecast.

So far, it is all good news for Mary. But what happens when she runs into the icy clutches of a powerful delay rune? That is exactly what happens when we turn to fuel (your issues). Perhaps this will help explain why Mary has not already resolved her dilemma. Because Isa was drawn to highlight Mary's issues, it is possible that Mary is a procrastinator. If this is the case, Isa is there to tell her that she needs to push ahead. Solving the dispute is not something to delay

CONTINUED
NEXT PAGE

camp fire, the dead branches loom more menacingly. Perhaps this is why Mary can no longer delay – the branches are ready to fall.

It is now time to see things from the neighbour's side. The air position stands for outside influences. In this case, that is most likely her opponent. The upright Thurisaz tells us that the neighbour has been building barriers and counting on his luck to keep problems at bay. Now things are coming into sharper focus. The neighbour may be relying on luck to keep the branches from falling on Mary's house, and the barrier of the trees may make him feel more protected and comfortable. If he cuts them, he may lose that barrier and feel exposed.

Is the solution to Mary's problem as simple as building a fence? With the trees pruned, Mary's house would be out of danger and the fence would maintain the

indefinitely. The other positive runes, especially the upright Tiwaz, tell her that now is the time to strike. Mary needs to overcome her natural tendency to delay. Isa is in the fuel position, so therefore it may be Mary's delaying tactics that have 'fuelled' this feud. Since wood is the primary fuel of a

neighbour's need for a barrier between their properties. This is something to mull over as we continue the reading.

When sitting around a camp fire, smoke can blow towards you, giving you an opaque obstacle to your enjoyment of the fire and the night air. In this runecast, smoke stands for obstacles. What is keeping Mary and her neighbour from finding a solution they can both live with? The upright Fehu, with its associations with money and wealth, just may provide an excellent clue. Pruning the trees and building a fence will both cost money. The neighbour may not have the funds necessary to make the improvements. If Mary offered to help pay for the fence, the neighbour might be far more inclined to agree to her solution. Fehu also counsels speaking with honesty, telling the neighbour how she really feels. Once he understands that she is afraid of damage to her property from the dead branches, and that it is not an attempt to demolish his barrier, he will probably feel the same way as she does.

Finally, we have arrived at ash – the future. When a fire is extinguished, what remains are ashes. That is the future of fire. Mary's future is portended by the rune Jera. Jera is a rune of justice, often legal in nature. We have also found out who the mysterious man with the advice is – a lawyer. If, during their conversation, Mary tells her

CONTINUED NEXT PAGE

neighbour that, legally, he is responsible for looking after the trees on his property, it might help to open his eyes. Mary is definitely in a position of strength on this one. The law stands behind her.

Jera is also a cycle rune, which predicts that the future for Mary is very positive. If Mary asks a lawyer for advice, and offers to help build a fence, the dispute will most probably be solved, with no hurt feelings on either side. Both neighbours will get what they want. Mary won't have the threat of the dead branches and the neighbour will have a new fence worked for his property.

It might seem as if I chose the runes consciously, manipulating the reading to get the 'right' runes in the right spots. I didn't. I drew them blindly, thinking only about Mary and her difficulty with her neighbour. If you are asked to give counsel using the runes, please be as honest as possible. Don't tell the person what you think they want to hear. Draw the runes blindly and let the stones give the answers. Trust your senses and the runes will make sense when you interpret them.

EIGHT-STONE READING: 'WHAT STEPS CAN I TAKE TO IMPROVE MY RELATIONSHIP?'

Relationships are one of the most important aspects of most people's lives and they are often the focus of questions for the runes. A good relationship layout usually includes stone positions for each of the two people involved. This eight-stone, heart-shaped layout is a good example of a relationship spread. The left side represents the feminine half of the relationship, and the right the masculine. Of course, not every relationship is between a man and a woman, so if you are using this layout for two people of the same gender, choose a side for each, and ignore the male and female aspect. Draw the stones in the order of the numbers beneath each position. It is not a simple clockwise placement.

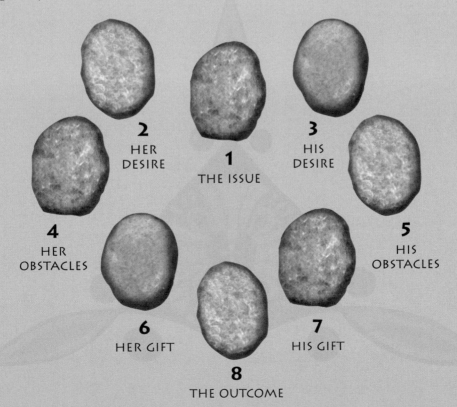

2
HER DESIRE

1
THE ISSUE

3
HIS DESIRE

4
HER OBSTACLES

5
HIS OBSTACLES

6
HER GIFT

7
HIS GIFT

8
THE OUTCOME

REVERSED ALGIZ, REVERSED OTHALA, SOWILO, REVERSED ANSUZ, DAGAZ, INGWAZ, HAGALAZ, UPRIGHT WUNJO

I have cast Diana and Steve as the principals, with Diana worrying that the spark has left their marriage and wondering what they can do to get it back. While thinking about this question, I drew the runes shown here.

Although the stones are mixed, the first thing you might notice is that Diana's side has two reversed stones, while none of the stones on Steve's side can be reversed. Are the problems her fault? Because this is not a simple yes or no question, you can't draw that conclusion. Let the runes tell you what is going on by reading about each in the order in which they were drawn.

In the first position, representing 'the issue', you will see a reversed Algiz. This indicates that somewhere between them is a source of dishonesty. It might be coming from Steve, or it might be coming from Diana, or it could even be coming from someone on the outside. At this point, we need to read more of the runes, to try to pin down what is going on between these two people so that we can find the source of the dishonesty.

In the desire positions, Diana has a reversed Othala and Steve has drawn Sowilo. The reversed Othala speaks of undue haste, alienation and the possibility that Diana is hiding her inner truths. It appears she is rushing towards achieving her desires and, in doing so, has damaged her relationship with Steve.

Because this is a paired read, you need to find out what Steve's desires are in

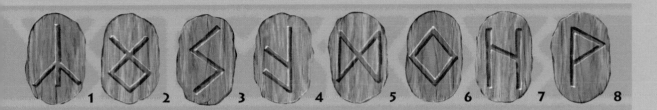

1   2   3   4   5   6   7   8

order to understand Diana's better. Sowilo is a rune of victory and robust health. It is a very positive and strong rune, but it does include some warnings. Steve is probably working too hard, going without relaxation and drowning in stress.

Putting these two together, it is not difficult to see why the couple are having problems. Both are running at top speed and probably have not given much time or thought to their relationship. Their desires are not focused on each other at all. They are geared towards speed and success without sufficient thought for one another.

Perhaps their obstacles will shed some further light on their difficulties. Diana has drawn a reversed Ansuz and Steve has Dagaz. Once again, Diana is faced with the spectre of lies and deceit. She may be getting bad advice, or is being tricked into doing

something that makes her uncomfortable. It is no wonder Diana asked for help from the runes. She probably didn't know where else to turn, nor whom to trust.

Steve, on the other hand, has the positive rune Dagaz. What obstacles is he facing? He's probably got some fear because he is on the cusp of a major change. Things are going well for him, most likely in his career. We have already seen that he is a workaholic, so his hard work is now paying off. But he has also got Hagalaz in his side of the reading, so he may be focusing too much on his problems.

In short, Diana continues to deal with dishonesty and Steve continues to be focused almost solely on his work. Neither of them appears to be supporting each other.

In a surprising turn, the 'gift' position gives us two unreversable runes, but this time it is Diana who gets the positive stone

CONTINUED

→

NEXT PAGE

and Steve who gets the rune with more negative connotations. Diana's gift is the rune Ingwaz. Suddenly, she is the one with the new beginning, the reduction of stress and completion. Because this is what Steve appears to need, it makes perfect sense that it would be Diana's gift. If he would give his wife a place in his life again, she could provide the answer to his overwhelming stress and tendency to work too hard.

Steve, on the other hand, has Hagalaz, a powerful delay rune. Hagalaz also speaks of disruptive outside forces. Could this be the dishonest person who is causing his wife such distress? If so, Steve's intervention could indeed be the gift Diana needs, if he will stop for long enough to notice her. Hagalaz is also a rune of new beginnings, although this time it is through disruption, instead of a natural cycle, like Diana's Ingwaz.

With both gifts being new beginnings, and each holding the key to reducing the stress of the other, it is becoming clear what this couple must do. They need to turn to each other, as they used to, for help and guidance. They must get off their roller-coasters and overly fast lifestyles, and carve out some time to be together. The problems in their marriage have a good chance of dissipating, if only

they would work together to find solutions to the problems they each individually face. Diana and Steve are each other's best answer, if only they would realize it.

If they follow the advice of the runes, the outcome is represented by the stone Wunjo. Wunjo is the rune of joy and success. What a marvellous stone to get in the result position of a runecast. With Wunjo in their future, they will both experience success in their careers, without the frantic speed and stress they are feeling now. It will also bring new energy to both of them. No more being stretched too far or dealing with delays. Wunjo also tells of the change both Diana and Steve found in their gift runes. This change is one of joy and closeness to family. By turning to each other in this time of crisis and relying on the gifts each of them brings to the marriage, Diana and Steve will achieve the happiness and closeness they both desire. What once was lost can now be found, if only they stop their frenetic lives long enough to reconnect with each other.

The dishonesty portended by the reversed Othala appears to be the lie that both can stand alone, and neither needs the other. They do need each other if they are to find happiness in both their work and their marriage. To guide your present life, as this example shows, the runes can bring out aspects that may have been hidden from you. They can illuminate problems and suggest solutions. An oracle, a portal, a guide – the runes will be whatever you need them to be.

USING RUNES TO EXPLORE YOUR FUTURE

Can runes predict the future? No. The runes can forecast a possible future, but primarily the runes are a means of bringing to light those issues and influences you need to be aware of in order to bring about positive changes. The future is yours to shape. That said, whenever someone uses a divinatory source, the thought 'What will the future bring?' remains. After all, if you could accurately predict the future, you would be able to avoid pitfalls and traps, take advantage of opportunities and guide your life towards goals with a fair degree of certainty. You would also know to be out of the house when your in-laws decide to pay a spontaneous visit.

The way to prepare for the future is to learn from your past and to guide your present. The runes are not tied to time. You can ask about your past, present and future, and you will receive guidance. You can ask about yourself or a friend. Your questions can be very precise or general. You can draw a single stone or a dozen. What your runes can tell you is limited only by your imagination and the time you spend with them.

In this section, I will introduce you to some more layouts, and the questions that we ask of the runes will be focused on the future. There is no need to use a crystal ball if you have the runes.

1 TODAY   **2** CHALLENGES   **3** ONE YEAR

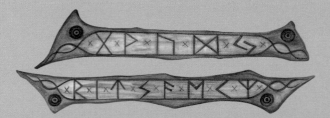

THREE-STONE READING: 'WHERE WILL I BE IN A YEAR'S TIME?'

Sometimes it helps to get a quick overview of where you might be heading. Will your life be the same in a year's time as it is today? If you continue on your current path, where will it lead? To get an answer, you can use a modified three-stone reading. In this layout, the 'today' rune is what is going on in your current life. The middle stone outlines the challenges you will meet and the final stone is the result (in one year's time), if you meet these challenges.

SAMPLE READING
REVERSED MANNAZ, UPRIGHT BERKANA, INGWAZ

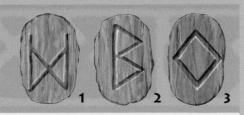

1   2   3

While doing a reading for Tim, I drew a reversed Mannaz in the today position. This rune warns that he is standing alone and may have an enemy. It also indicates the possibility of someone foreign entering his life.

Happily, things improve immediately with an upright Berkana in the challenges position. This rune of family, fertility and intuition shows a strong path out of the suspicion and loneliness of the reversed Mannaz. Tim needs to fill his life with

CONTINUED → NEXT PAGE

people he can trust, such as family members or friends who are as close as family. There is a sense of rebirth with Berkana and this could mean that to escape his current problems, he needs to look at making some changes. A new line of work, a new female companion or perhaps a new attitude towards his own life might help Tim escape from the dark times he is currently experiencing.

This interpretation is heavily reinforced by the cyclical rune, Ingwaz, landing in the result position. It also speaks of a new

beginning and assures fruitful success if Tim is willing to do the work. By divesting himself of the negative forces in his current life, Tim will be challenged to start anew. If he does so, by this time next year he will reap the rewards.

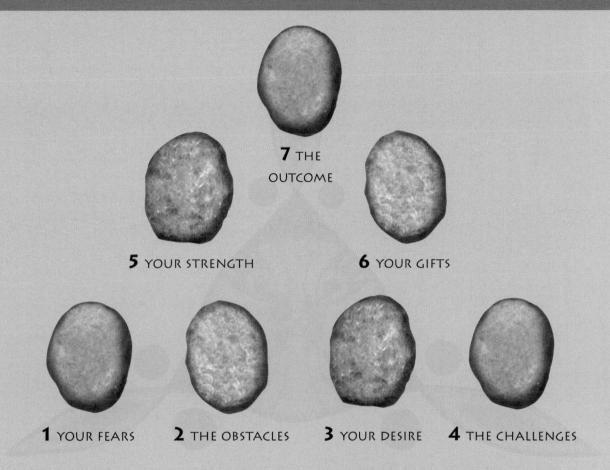

7 THE OUTCOME

5 YOUR STRENGTH

6 YOUR GIFTS

1 YOUR FEARS

2 THE OBSTACLES

3 YOUR DESIRE

4 THE CHALLENGES

SEVEN-STONE READING:
'HOW CAN I MANIFEST ABUNDANCE?'

There are times when you want to know how to achieve certain goals. A future-centric layout is an excellent choice in a situation like this. For example, if you wanted to find someone to love, to change jobs or to get on to more solid financial ground, you might consider trying a Pyramid Goal spread. This layout begins at the bottom (follow the numbers to see the order in which the stones are drawn) with things you will need to know in order to change your future. Above those stones are what you bring to the equation and, finally, there is the result stone, or outcome.

REVERSED ANSUZ, HAGALAZ, REVERSED MANNAZ, EIHWAZ, UPRIGHT URUZ, UPRIGHT NAUTHIZ, ISA

In this example, Janet wants to know how she can manifest abundance. She does not have enough money to live comfortably, is single and has not shown much ambition in her life.

This is a pretty negative reading, but honesty is extremely important when drawing runes. Throwing back stones because they are not what you hoped for won't do any good. Sometimes you will get bad news. Remember that the negative aspects are just as important, if not more so, than the positive. If you are seeking guidance and change, then negative reads will focus on what it is in your life that needs to be looked at closely.

Janet's reading begins with a reversed Ansuz in the fear position. By reading about Ansuz you will note that it speaks of someone giving bad advice. There are lies and deceit. However, keep in mind that this is Janet's fear – it may be that she has major trust issues. Her intuition is not tuned in to whether people are lying or telling the truth, and therefore she has been burned several times by bad advice, lies, deceit and dishonesty. She needs to be more aware.

With that in mind, we look at the obstacles. Hagalaz, a stone with no reverse, stands in that position. A powerful delay rune, Hagalaz stands for the disruption and destruction of outside forces. It is understandable why this landed in the obstacles position – disruptive outside forces would be powerful obstacles indeed. It is also possible that someone, and not something, is

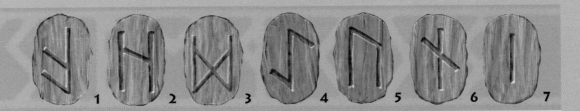

1 2 3 4 5 6 7

the disruptive force. Could it be the untrustworthy person portended by the reversed Ansuz? We need to continue reading the stones to find out.

Janet's desire is represented by a reversed Mannaz. This same stone showed up in the last reading we did, and, sure enough, it speaks of Janet standing alone among enemies. Why would this be her wish? The truth is we don't always want what is best for us. Smoking can be a deadly habit, yet people still do it. Some people thrive on danger, risking their lives for an adrenaline rush. Most likely, Janet has trust issues and therefore sets herself apart, fearing enemies and dishonest interactions. For Janet to manifest more abundance, she may have to deal with her own internal issues first. Yet, before we draw any conclusions, let's see what else she has in her reading.

In the challenges position, she has Eihwaz, the rune that represents the yew tree. The challenge appears to be one of strength and flexibility. Janet can no longer be her usual rigid, untrusting self. She needs to put her strength into more fruitful pursuits, instead of spending it on mistrust and isolationism. For someone with so many fears, this is indeed a challenge. The next stone, the strength stone, will be very telling.

CONTINUED
NEXT PAGE

SAMPLE READING
CONTINUED:

Having Uruz in the strength position shows that Janet has a lot to draw on. Uruz is a very strong rune and is made doubly so from its position in the runecast. This shows that Janet has all the tools she needs to manifest abundance. She is healthy, is able to work hard and has the strength and stamina she needs. It is becoming apparent that the only thing holding Janet back is Janet herself.

This becomes even more pronounced when we see that her gifts rune is Nauthiz. This powerful delay rune may be difficult to see as a gift. However, by adding what we have already learned about Janet, it becomes clearer. Her ability to delay and avoid is well honed. This means that although she has the strength to conquer any problem, she is far more likely to engage in avoidance behaviour. If you delay for long enough, problems and opportunities may disappear. Janet has relied on this in the past and probably hopes that abundance will come if she is patient enough. In short, Janet has exiled herself to a 'waiting place', hoping that the world will hand her what she desires so that she won't have to venture out among her imagined enemies.

The outcome then becomes clear: Isa, the hard, cold ice of delay. Until Janet uses her prodigious strength to go after her goals, the delays will continue. Abundance is not going to drop into her lap, yet that is all Janet is willing to hope for. She wants the rewards without the work and the runes tell her that this will not happen. She needs to use her abilities in order to manifest abundance. Otherwise, it will be locked away, frozen and unreachable.

ELEVEN-STONE READING: 'WHAT CAN I DO TO ACHIEVE MY GOALS?'

Your life's goals probably occupy many of your thoughts. Getting guidance about them is something the runes can offer. For this question, an in-depth layout involving eleven stones is an excellent choice.

This reading will give you the kind of detail that you will need in order to achieve your personal goals. The number beneath each stone indicates the order in which to pull the runes. The spread begins on the bottom left, with two stones representing your past. From there, you can see a virtual wall of stones separating you from your future. These are the traits you bring and the influences at play. They may be standing between you and your goals, or they could be what will help you achieve them. Finally, in the upper right, we see the possible future.

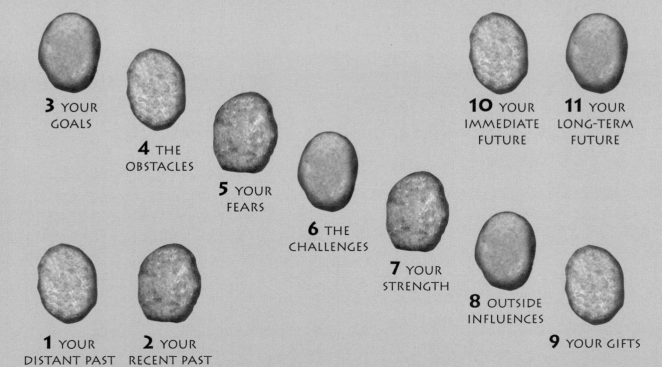

3 YOUR GOALS

4 THE OBSTACLES

5 YOUR FEARS

6 THE CHALLENGES

7 YOUR STRENGTH

8 OUTSIDE INFLUENCES

9 YOUR GIFTS

10 YOUR IMMEDIATE FUTURE

11 YOUR LONG-TERM FUTURE

1 YOUR DISTANT PAST

2 YOUR RECENT PAST

SAMPLE READING

ISA, UPRIGHT LAGUZ, GEBO, DAGAZ, UPRIGHT BERKANA, UPRIGHT EHWAZ, REVERSED URUZ, UPRIGHT ANSUZ, UPRIGHT MANNAZ, REVERSED KENAZ, UPRIGHT WUNJO

David recently got married and is now concerned about his future at the law firm where he works. He and his wife, Cindy, want to have a family and he wants to be able to provide for them in a comfortable and abundant way. Right now, David's job is not very exciting. It is an entry-level position and he is ambitious. David wants to know how he can achieve his career goals – partnership and a good salary – so that he can provide for his new wife and future family. Concentrating on David's question, I drew the runes shown here.

Immediately, it is easy to spot how wonderfully positive this reading is going to be. Almost all of the stones are upright, and many of the runes are strong, positive influences. It looks as though David has what it takes to achieve his goals. But, to guide him on that journey, he needs to know the

specific things that will aid and inhibit him, so that he can properly prepare himself.

Beginning in the bottom left corner, David's distant past is represented by the delay rune, Isa. Most likely he had a slow start, unsure of what he wanted to do for a living. However, things changed when he met Cindy. Laguz, a strong female rune, sits in the recent past. David's wife has obviously had a strong influence on him. Laguz also portends that David's life is going to have a new, positive direction. That is a wonderful omen, indeed. David's creativity is strong, as is Cindy's influence on him. This young couple is prepared to meet new challenges and carve out the life they desire. But what will they encounter on their way?

David's goals are expressed in the gift rune, Gebo. This is the rune of partnerships, and in this case it seems pretty clear that one

important partnership in David's life is the one he shares with Cindy. Because Gebo landed in the goals position, however, it affirms David's own goal of some day becoming a partner in the law firm where he works. Drawing this rune was incredibly portentous for David. If he is willing to work hard and give the firm his loyalty and best efforts, then he has an excellent chance of becoming a partner.

What obstacles are going to be placed in the way of achieving these goals? The positive rune, Dagaz, sits in that position. Dagaz promises security and success. In what way is that an obstacle? Most likely, these are issues with David. He may be so

focused on making a success of his career, and the security that will give him, that he obsesses about them. To remove these obstacles, he needs to stop worrying so much and allow things to happen naturally. He has so many advantages that he doesn't need to be obsessed with his career. Rather than fretting about being a partner, he should be putting his energy into his current work. The better he does his job now, the better he will appear to the people who have the power to advance his career.

What is David afraid of? Berkana is in his fear position, and, because it is a strong feminine fertility rune, it would not be out of line to think that David has more than one fear around the prospect of starting a family. It is very possible that Cindy is the one who wants to have children right away. David may have agreed to it, but in his heart he is

CONTINUED

NEXT PAGE

SAMPLE READING CONTINUED:

1   2   3

probably harbouring a lot of fear. Will he be a good father? Will he be able to provide for and protect his children? What if he makes a mistake? Because Berkana is upright, David has the tools to fight these fears. With Cindy's help, he will prevail. David's life is ready for a new phase, a new beginning. Having children will only enhance their lives together.

What challenges will David face in light of this new beginning? The upright Ehwaz should give some good insight. When you read about this rune, you will note how positive it sounds. David and Cindy will strengthen their relationship, David will get a promotion – but where are the challenges? Few things in this world are without challenges, even if they are the very things you want most. If David gets a promotion, he will have more responsibility. He may have

to work longer hours and this could put a strain on his young marriage. The important thing for him to remember is that he will be able to meet these challenges. The upright Ehwaz is an excellent indication that he has what it takes to be challenged and prevail.

Now we arrive at one of David's two reversed stones: Uruz. Uruz is a strength rune, and yet it landed reversed in the strength position of the reading. It is very possible that David has issues with low self-esteem and thinks of himself as weak. Because Gebo and Laguz are in the reading, Cindy may be the stronger of the two. David sees her strength and allows her to push him into things he feels he is not ready for. Perhaps things are going a little too fast for David. Talk of promotions and children so soon after getting his job and getting married may be leaving David feeling powerless.

4 5 6 7 8 9 10 11

Because the rest of his reading is so overwhelmingly positive, David will have the ability to fight these moments of weakness. In fact, these lapses may be needed. If he did not have them, he could be seen as arrogant and threatening. That is how a weakness becomes a strength. David can remain humble despite his gifts and that will help to draw people to him.

In the outside influences position we find the rune Ansuz. It makes a lot of sense that this advice rune landed in this position. Someone in a position of authority will offer David advice and guidance. He should take the advice, because it may be the key to his advancement in the law firm. If an older lawyer takes him under his wing, David's rise in the firm could begin. This older adviser may also be able to shore up David's self-esteem through praise.

This ties in with the next stone, Mannaz. This rune of interdependence also speaks of advice, but, because this is in David's gifts position, it shows that he is a good listener and will take the advice given. It also reinforces the idea that David's humility and non-judgemental attitudes are gifts that others appreciate.

The stage is now set. You have seen David's past and now know which things, both positive and negative, will influence his future. It is time to see what that future might be.

The reversed Kenaz in the immediate future portends a loss of some kind. It does not have to

CONTINUED → NEXT PAGE

be a damaging loss, especially since the bulk of his reading was positive. For example, if Cindy gets pregnant they will lose the carefree lifestyle of a childless couple. Babies need a lot of attention and care, and David may feel himself resenting so much of Cindy's focus being taken away from him, but this loss will pale in relation to the gain of a new child. It could also be a loss in his job. If he does get a promotion, he may miss some aspects of his old position, such as the shorter hours or the lack of responsibility. But he will gain so much more that this loss will be small in comparison. Losses don't have to be bad and with a positive reading it is important to put the few negative signposts into perspective.

We have come to the final stone. What is David's long-term future? There is no better rune to find in the result position than the joy rune, Wunjo. Wunjo in the long-term future position predicts a number of positive things. David will have happiness in his work and in his family. Promotions will come, as will children, and David's goals will be met.

An upright Wunjo is such a positive celebration of life that it is the perfect rune to find at the end of this long and positive read. David and Cindy have a lot going for them. If they follow the advice of the runes, work hard, honour each other and their work, rely on each other's strengths and shore up each other's weaknesses, their lives will be filled with long-term joy.

CONCLUSION

You now have all the tools you need to read the runes. If you are faced with a difficult decision, feel unsure of yourself or the direction in which you are going or just want to have a little fun, you can call on the runes. As long as you remember that they are just a guide, you should have a long and healthy relationship with them.

When your friends find out that you can read runes, they will probably want you to answer some questions for them. It is up to you whether you want to do this or not. Your runes, especially if you made them yourself, are tied to your energy, so be sure of your answer. I enjoy reading the runes for others, because I know how helpful they have been for me. My only advice is to be honest. Don't flip a stone because it came out reversed and you don't want to deliver bad news. Don't throw a stone back because 'that one's no fun'. The only way you can be of any help to your friends is to be honest at all times, in every reading.

Here's hoping that your life is filled with Wunjo!

INDEX

ACKNOWLEDGEMENTS

Executive Editor Sandra Rigby
Editor Charlotte Wilson
Executive Art Editor Sally Bond
Designer Elizabeth Healey
Illustrators Jo Donegan, KJA-artists.com
Production Controller Louise Hall

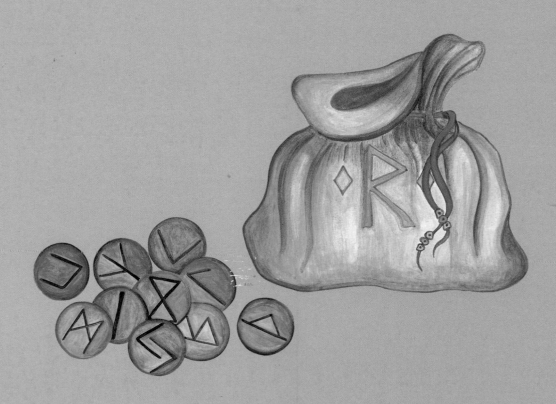